# The Complex Buddhist

DOING GOOD IN A CHALLENGING WORLD

# The Complex Buddhist

DOING GOOD IN A CHALLENGING WORLD

Ron Schultz

with a Foreword by

Richard Reoch
Special Envoy to the Sakyong of Shambhala

**EMERGENT**™
P U B L I C A T I O N S

The Complex Buddhist:
Doing Good in a Challenging World
Written by: Ron Schultz

Library of Congress Control Number: 2015960150

ISBN: 978-1-938158-17-9

Copyright © 2015
Emergent Publications,
3810 N. 188th Ave, Litchfield Park, AZ 85340, USA

Printed in the United States of America

# About the Author

Ron Schultz has written, co-written and edited 25 published books on social innovation, emergence, and entrepreneurship. In 2014, he received the Social Innovation Leadership Award from the World CSR Congress. His other books include: *Adjacent Opportunities —Sparking Emergent Social Action* (Emergent Publications, 2010); *Creating Good Work—The World's Leading Social Entrepreneurs Show How to Build a Healthy Economy* (Palgrave Macmillan, 2013); *The Mindful Corporation: Liberating the Human Spirit at Work* (with Paul Nakai) (Leadership Press, 2000); and *Open Boundaries: Creating Business Innovation through Complexity* (with Howard Sherman) (Perseus Books, 1998).

Ron is the co-founder of Waterman Aylsworth, LLC and founder of Red Tiger & Associates, and Entrepreneurs4 Change, organizations dedicated to mindfulness-based social innovation and entrepreneurship. He has been a Shambhala practitioner for 25 years and a meditation instructor for the past 15.

His current columns, Adjacent Opportunities and Creating Good Work, appear in the journal, *Emergence: Complexity and Organization* and on *CSRwire*, respectfully.

# Contents

# Acknowledgements

Abook like this owes a great deal to many folks who have influenced and participated in its development. First, I'd like to recognize Johana Sanderford-Schultz, my elder daughter, for doing such a wonderful job of helping me organize and edit this book. Her critical analysis and keen eye helped shape this rather disparate gathering of pieces into a very readable and collected whole. And her uncanny ability to discern the confusing from the confused and right the course is greatly appreciated.

I would also like to express my undying love and appreciation to Laura Sanderford, my wife, the mother of Johana and our younger daughter, Emily, who is also my executive producer and the love of my life. Laura was always the first to read all of these pieces before they found their way into print and have her cogent and guiding say about them. Laura is an exemplary educator and a brilliant light in my life.

I also want to acknowledge my dear friend and publisher, Kurt Richardson, who has been willing to leap into the fray again and again, providing me with over a decade's worth of opportunities to share these ideas and frame these discussions. Kurt has built Emergent Publications into a cutting-edge publishing house that is not cowed by convention or limited by bias and tradition. For that I am forever grateful.

It is also imperative that I thank Michael Lissack for his friendship, loyalty and brilliant mind. Over our 20 years of friendship and involvement in the world of complexity, Michael has helped form my thinking, supported my family and been a great friend. Without him, Emergent Publications would have never seen the light of day, nor would its many authors found such a formidable home for their ideas.

As to the list of people who added to this collection, and there will invariably be omissions, I will mention a group that includes my life-long friend and constant advisor, Les Forman, my colleague and ever-perceptive friend, Stephen Heffernan, my business partner at Waterman Aylsworth and impeccable Buddhist scholar, Mark Allen, my colleague in mindfulness-based emotional intelligence and baseball commissary, John Parsons, and Richard Clar, whose artistic vision stretches beyond the boundaries of the Earth itself, demonstrating that the possible is bounded only by our imagination.

I would also like to recognize the folks at CSRwire, who have provided a platform for some of these pieces that have moved their boundaries as well. They have been a great and open partner since 2013, and I am grateful for their support and openness to ideas that extend beyond traditional corporate responsibility.

Finally, I would like to acknowledge my teacher, the Sakyong Mipham Rinpoche, and the worldwide Shambhala community he leads. For nearly a quarter century, this community has provided me with a warmth and cheerfulness that has afforded a deep and penetrating realization of the world as it is. The Sakyong, which means Earth Protector, has demonstrated again and again that we can create an enlightened society by being and modeling the example we want others to emulate.

With a deep bow of gratitude and appreciation, I thank all of those folks who have tolerated my silliness, endured my jokes, and been patient with those places in which I still get stuck. It is not difficult to realize how important the simple act of accommodating others is to the healthiness of our lives together. Thank you Thank you.

# Foreword

This is a book for people who need strong hearts in dark times. I was online when its author, Ron Schultz, sent it to me. Congress had just voted to block the resettlement of Syrian and Iraqi refugees in the the United States.  "Our first priority is to protect the American people," said House Speaker Paul D. Ryan.  I was online trying to get a rough idea of the various levels of threat that US citizens are facing.

*The New York Times* keeps a regular update of terrorist bombings. I started there and also looked up all the various forms of terror attacks that had taken place world-wide up to that point in 2015.  There were 289 bombings, shootings, stabbings and other incidents.

In order to get some kind of comparison with the threat possibly facing US nationals, I looked for details of all people from Western nations, including Israel and the West Bank, Russia and Turkey, who had been killed. I did not include people stabbed or injured or assailants slain by the security forces. Westerners died during attacks in Australia, Bosnia and Herzegovina, Denmark, Egypt, France, Israel and the West Bank, Tunisia, and Turkey.  The death toll was 589. That included the November blood-bath in Paris.

I then looked up gun deaths in the United States for the same period: 11,681.

Even allowing for errors in reporting, or a somewhat arbitrary definition of "westerners", or failing to mention the hundreds of similar deaths in Africa, Asia, the rest of the Middle East and North Africa, or leaving out civilian deaths caused by aerial bombardment in Afghanistan, Iraq, Syria and Yemen, the statistics are a startling reminder—if one be needed—that we are all living in dangerous times.

So what's the connection between my online statistics and the arrival of Ron Schultz's book? They are both about fear. The nature of fear, the consequences of fear and the way we deal with fear. That's what makes these pages timely, relevant and challenging to all of us.

Please don't think that Buddhists are immune from this.

I don't mean immune from being attacked. It's obvious that we can all be the victims of indiscriminate assaults at any time. I mean: don't think Buddhists are immune from being crazed by fear and hatred. Our own people are involved in extremist crimes as well. I have personal experience of this from my work in South and Southeast Asia, particularly in the Buddhist countries of Myanmar (formerly Burma) and Sri Lanka.

This was one of the issues confronted by Buddhist leaders from across North America when we were invited to gather at the White House in May 2015. At that point, an estimated 88,000 men, women and children had fled in unseaworthy boats from Myanmar becoming what Time magazine called "The Nowhere People". Thousands are believed to have perished along the way. Survivors testify to rape and torture.

Most are members of a minority Muslim community, the Rohingya, who have been the victims of vicious attacks by Buddhists, fuelled by the inflammatory hate speeches of nationalist monks. The leader of the country's extremist 969 Movement, Bhikkhu Wirathu, described in the media as the Face of Buddhist Terror, is said to have styled himself "the Buddhist bin Laden."

The previous year I had been in Sri Lanka at the time of the country's worst intercommunal rioting in more than 30 years. Extremist Buddhists attacked long-standing Muslim communities in the south of the island. In a speech before the assault, the leader of the self-styled "Buddhist Power Force", the monk Gnanasara Thero, told the crowd that they had been accused of being racists. He screamed, "Yes we are!" to a roar of approval from thousands of his supporters.

I mention all this grim news because it is tempting to think that the Buddhist message of peace, compassion and social well-being is somehow simple, straightforward and something we can take for granted. In fact it is not a message we can take for granted at all. That's why this book talks about "The Complex Buddhist".

On the surface it may seem that this book—dealing with the challenges of social innovation, ethical entrepreneurship, and the art of deep collaboration—is a far cry from headlines about refugees, street violence, extremism and war. It's not. It invites us to acknowledge and contemplate the seeds that take root in our unexamined attitudes and behaviours. For among those seeds are those that later give rise to the familiar patterns of mistrust, conflict and frustration. So often, these bedevil even the greatest and most inspiring of human endeavours.

At the same time it is possible for other seeds to blossom. They also arise from—and are sustained by—our deep patterns of feeling, thought and behaviour. But they offer a very different way forward. Thus, this book is not only about fear. It is also about courage, compassion and societal creativity.

In this way, the contemplations in these pages are not merely something we can benefit from in our lives, work and organizations. They also offer a kind of inner "boot-camp" for peace workers. What we find is both heart-warming and unsettling—an invitation to shift not only the way we think about things, but how we behave. Ron reminds us:

*When we shift our perception of each other—how we see each other, our understanding of the models we might have created about each other—we must also shift the rules that we have put in place for ourselves that govern how we relate. If we shift our understanding but don't shift the rules that govern our behavior, nothing changes and nothing new will emerge.*

When he turns to "dissolving cultural intransigence", the relation between the atrocities we are living through and our own deep-seated fears becomes startlingly clear. He writes:

*Within the realm of emergent phenomena, one of the most insidious combinations is prejudice and its fraternal twin, bigotry. Both arise out of the interaction between our fear and ignorance. Our inability to assimilate something being different than us or our experience of the world in which we live. Few of us are immune and many make a common practice out of it. And from that, our global society suffers under the further emergence of hatred, terror, and mistrust. It is a cycle that has continued since the dawn of what we call "consciousness."*

The way out of this ancient labyrinth is not through blame, either of ourselves or others. It is through the insight that arises out of working with ourselves and engaging profoundly with others—echoing the other part of this book's title: "Doing Good in a Challenging World."

Perhaps it was exactly this kind of self-reflection, inner work and socially transformative enterprise that the Buddha had in mind when he told his earliest disciples:

*Go forth for the good of the many, for the happiness of the many, with compassion towards the world, for the benefit, the welfare and the happiness of all humanity and the gods.*

Richard Reoch
Special Envoy to the Sakyong of Shambhala
London, England

# Preface

The great joy in writing a preface is that the author of the same has the privilege of identifying anecdotes, stories, and, sometimes, aphorisms which capture the essence of why a book should be read—while leaving the hard work of fleshing out those very same things to the author of the actual book. Ron Schultz makes this preface author's task even more joyous in that *The Complex Buddhist: Doing Good in a Challenging World* itself is a book of stories—stories of wisdom, where anecdotes cannot do the central themes justice. I am left with mere aphorisms, and it becomes the task of you, dear reader, to flesh these out with Ron's help.

Begin with **respect context and remember the context of respect**. To respect context is to approach each story with the understanding that you will visit it multiple times. Each time you do so, the context and inner stories you bring to the written story will differ, because time will have passed and the context of **you** will be different. What will be the same is the notion of respect—of viewing again.

Then think back to the sage words of Winston Churchill during World War II as he described the importance of a physical context, when rebuilding the House of Commons building, after it had been bombed, was the subject of public debate. Churchill stated "**We shape our buildings, and afterwards our buildings shape us**." As with physical contexts, which we revisit and respect, the same is true for narrative and cognitive contexts. The stories in *The Complex Buddhist* are shaped, in part, by how you the reader read them, and then, in turn, how you process, embody, and enact the lessons you extract from those same stories will help to shape the future you.  And, the cycle will repeat.

The cycle of story, interpretation, relation to context, and re-understood story serves the function of Churchill's buildings.  In that sense, the cycle is like a black box—the logical kind (not the airplane kind) where we observe inputs and outputs, but what goes on in the middle is hidden.  We, nonetheless, draw inferences from the patterns we observe as the inputs and outputs take place.  In drawing those inferences, we attempt to "explain" the mystery of the black box itself.  Ranulph Glanville's aphorism "**inside every black box is a white box yearning to be free**" becomes an apt lesson.  In respecting context, we see a black box, it speaks to us, and as we each apply our own context to it, we try to whiten the box and release its mysteries.

In that cycle, Humberto Maturana's famous aphorism "**Everything said is said to and by an observer**" itself gets enacted.  Ron will function as the initial observer, and then you observe his observations.  In doing so, you process your own lessons and your own insights—such that when the story is retold by you, its context has changed and so too has its observations.  In effect, the story has observed you and altered its lessons in light of your context.  When done right it is a cycle of mutual respect, and Ron's columns herein make it easy to be done right.

The aphorisms aptly describe the key insights of *The Complex Buddhist*, but they also describe the key insights of cybernetics and pragmatic constructivism. A main lesson from cybernetics is what is called Ashby's Law of Requisite Variety: "**The controller of a system must have at least as many degrees of freedom as the system**

***desiring to be controlled."*** Ron's complex Buddhism would counter this with the observations that systems cannot be "controlled," that the desire for control lies with the observer, and that degrees of freedom is as much a description of both the model or narrative told about a system as it is about the system itself. If you can remember these observations as you read The *Complex Buddhist*, you will have a powerful tool with which to give Ron's columns the context of respect which they deserve and which they, in turn, will mirror to you, the reader.

As regards this book, you are not a controller, but an observer and an active participant in your life outside it. You are both the provider of context for how the stories are read, respected and the enactment of the context itself—as your ***self***.

In sharing these columns with us and with you, Ron is offering observations for you to observe further. How you embody them, how you enact them, the lessons you extract from their black boxes, whatever means of whitening you find that works for you, Ron's lessons become a part of you and the cycle continues.

May the cycle offer you some wisdom to build upon and to offer others.

Such is my goal for your reading of The *Complex Buddhist*.

Michael Lissack

Executive Director of the

Institute for the Study of Coherence and Emergence,

President of the American Society for Cybernetics

# Introduction

I n 1992, two powerful approaches to looking at the world exactly as it is showed-up in my life. I had known about each for years, but at this point in time, they both walked in the door and made themselves comfortable in what I call *my* life. One: the sciences of complexity and its attendant complex adaptive systems, and Two: Tibetan Buddhism. Seemingly the strangest of bedfellows, but actually more closely akin than certainly I first thought in 1992.

And while Buddhist teachings warn against systems of thinking that one can embrace and thereby limit one's capacity to be open to the world as it truly is, Complexity is, ultimately, like Buddhism, about being comfortable with the uncertainty and ambiguity with which we are often met. Both are also about how the world is, not how we want or expect it to show-up. And while one defines itself as science, and the other as a spiritual way of being, the distinction as we dig deeper is very thin.

*The Complex Buddhist—Doing Good in a Challenging World*, however, is not an attempt to chip away at the veneer that separates them, but rather, it's a series of observations about how these two work together and can inform our lives. I have had the great opportunity and privilege, for over a decade now, to write about how these two forces have helped me meet the world. In doing so, I have been able to explore their relationship and dig into how they work and interact, together.

Kurt Richardson, the publisher of Emergent Publications and the *E:CO* journal, has basically given me free reign to unleash this rather personal exploration on his reading audience. Neither of us really knew what might emerge from this concoction, but perhaps our lack of knowledge allowed us to take the plunge without getting too serious about the outcome. Of course, anyone who knows us also knows that taking either of us too seriously is far from a lasting proposition. Kurt's great sense of humor and his brilliance as a complex brewmeister has allowed this process to delve more fearlessly into the mixing of these potent elixirs. He has also made sure we didn't become too intoxicated by our own cleverness.

The process of self-organization always requires some sort of boundaries, even though Buddhism is quite comfortable without them. And so the relationship emerges and evolves.

My interest in Complexity and Buddhism found its initial ground in the early 80s when Nobel Physicist Murray Gell-Mann told me everything I knew was wrong, and that the answers I wanted would be found among the complex adaptive system scientists. I hate to admit it, but to a certain degree Murray was right.

I had begun my Buddhist practice in the early 90s, but it was because of Gell-Mann's advice that I eventually met my mentor, friend and co-author, Howard Sherman, with whom I wrote *Open Boundaries* (Perseus Books) in 1997. The book was a way to language the emerging sciences of complexity within a context that could be applied to organizations and enterprises. Then three years later, when Senn-Delaney Leadership provided me and Paul Nakei with the opportunity to write and publish *The Mindful Corporation* (Leadership Press) in 2000, it was my first attempt to bridge the gap, if one existed, between my Buddhist practice and my complexity education.

It was not too surprising that shortly after the publication of these seminal works in my understanding that I was introduced to social entrepreneurship. The progression, in my mind made perfect sense. A) if one understands how things emerge, then B) one is willing and able to meet whatever shows up exactly as it does, then C) finding solutions to pressing social issues has to follow. Well, at least the progression made sense in my mind.

*The Complex Buddhist* is actually the second collection of my essays Emergent Publications has published. The first, *Adjacent Opportunities: Sparking Emergent Social Action*, introduced my proclivity to what is often characterized as doing well by doing good. I will say, however, the doing well part has not always led the way, and my very patient wife, Laura, will certainly attest to that. But the doing good aspect has been worth every moment spent. And as my friend and colleague Stephen Heffernan helped me see, there is a significant difference between doing well and well-doing. I can live with that distinction.

What follows then are a series of pieces that have appeared in either *E:CO* or CSRwire, another publication that has given me license for the past few years to explore these ideas. Of course, publishing these essays as a single collection, implies that there might be a certain linearity within the assemblage. This presents a bit of a challenge, especially since both Buddhism and Complexity are non-linear in their nature. So, I confess, while attention was paid to the flow of the pieces that follow, they are connected as much by intention as they are content.

I will also say that while my thinking on these topics has been greatly influenced by dear and trusted advisors throughout the years in which these were written—

including but not limited to: Howard Sherman, Laura Sanderford (to whom I owe far more than this brief mention) Michael Lissack, Stephen Heffernan, Les Forman, the Sakyong Mipham Rinpoche, Dzongsar Kheyntse Rinpoche, Mark Allen, and Craig Dunn--how these ideas have been shaped herein is wholly my responsibility. I can blame none of these wonderful folks for how these ideas have been presented or been misconstrued.

From the notions of Engaged Emergence that introduces this slim volume, to the happiness and well-being ideas that close it, they are all part of the complex nature of this thing we refer to as our mind. And it is, without recourse that I must mention, at this time, Difflugia Arcellinida, a single-celled critter to which I was introduced to this summer by Michael Turvey and Claudia Carello. Difflugia have no brains and subsequently, by common definition, no minds, and yet they are capable of constructing an amazingly beautiful fluted house for themselves from found objects. Their emergent innovations are not based on brain-power. The lesson of Difflugia for me means that our thinking is greatly over-rated and undoubtedly misunderstood. And I would say that a Buddhist would undoubtedly agree with that single-celled critter.

In spite of this knowledge and to a certain degree because of it, I have compiled this collection I'm calling *The Complex Buddhist: Doing Good in a Challenging World*. May it benefit many.

# Engaged Emergence—Getting Beyond Enterprise Fortune Telling

Cause, condition, and effect characterize the process of emergence, but often times, rather than focusing on this, enterprises would rather spend billions trying to predict and divine what is going to happen in the future. How effective has this fortune telling been? The answer is costly and not very accurate. However, that fact hasn't seemed to stop anyone from investing more resources into enterprise soothsayers as a means of getting a leg up, no matter how inaccurate they prove to be.

If enterprises better understood what drives and influences business action, they might be a bit more successful in their prognostication by narrowing their sooth and recognizing the cues, as my colleague Michael Lissack would call them, that present themselves to those who, in fact can, see them as cues. This ability is what I am calling Engaged Emergence.

Engaged Emergence is attending to the resonance of the world, of which we are a part, and being authentically present to witness the auspicious coincidence of what emerges. In some cultures, this is also called mindfulness, our ability to focus our minds without distraction on what presents itself. The opposite of mindfulness is mindfilledness, a quality that is in constant distraction, and by its nature, will miss any but the most blatant cues that become present. The process begins with theory.

The Theory of Enterprise Action is based primarily on two core ingredients; 1) What we want—that which informs all our products and services, and can then be referred to as information, and 2) What we build to support getting what we want, or infrastructure. When the ratio between information and infrastructure is right, according to the given situation of the enterprise, the action takes place, successfully. When the ratio is not correct, and there is too much or too little infrastructure to support the acquisition of information, we do not get a successful action. Ah, if it were as simple as just that. Unfortunately, the actions we take in our enterprises are also influenced by two other forces: 1) The culture of the enterprise—a culture of fear automatically creates greater infrastructure to protect oneself from what is feared. A culture that is too loosey-goosey creates action that is too unbounded so that no organization, self or otherwise, can take place, and efforts dissipate. And then 2) Outside of the internal cultural influence there is the impact of the world at large that operates outside the control of the enterprise. This is the stuff of meltdowns.

The ability to recognize the available cues before a meltdown emerges can save valuable resources. If we are distracted by the causes and conditions before the meltdown, we will be unable to incorporate what presents itself in a fashion that will avoid disaster. Engaged Emergence is about being present enough to see what is emerging as it emerges.

Which is less costly—predicting what doesn't happen and/or missing what does, or seeing what's happening as it emerges and being able to incorporate it into present action? Engaged Emergence is attending to the cause and condition and then being able to witness the effect and respond accordingly. Mind-filled action is getting caught in the cause and condition and becoming a victim of the effect because it cannot be seen until after it has happened.

What is possible when we can make decisions by facing what emerges as it becomes known? What benefit arises from that ability to be present? When we operate in the world as it happens, the possible is actual. There is no separation. This is also not a mystical occurrence. It is the meeting place where resources not only afford the emergence of the new and novel, but also the same place where new and novel resources can also emerge.

Now it may seem that to be able to recognize these events as they transpire requires a certain clairvoyant capability, but as my colleague Dr. Les Forman explained, that is not the case. Much like a psychotherapist, it does require us to be able to listen from a place that psychodynamic therapists call free floating attention. And, we're not going to operate effectively within this possibility space if we are already mind-filled. At its core, every emergent action takes place within the context of our ability to articulate it, so in order to deliver the message of what we see, we must not only witness it we must also be able to hear how it manifests itself so we can express it. If we can't listen with the appropriate capacity to grasp the message, if our minds are too distracted, it may mean that we miss the opportunity.

In honing this faculty to become engaged observers of the world in front of us and spot the cues that point us in the direction of new possibilities, we can also miss the opportunity if we limit our observations to strategic issues or the next hot item. Enterprise leaders often think they know what outcomes they want to take place and so they keep their focus and approach purely strategic. However, if we are actively opening our perceptions to the emergent opportunities that may make themselves available, we must also be ready to broaden our vision to include new outcomes that may arise and be required to satisfy the real need of the enterprise. This is a significant departure from the thinking that, as a matter of course, we define outcomes and goals and then create strategies to meet those outcomes. It compels us to rework our attachments to traditional outcomes as our only choices, and transform them, to say, focus on development rather than growth. The notion of growth, while certainly appealing to a short-term vision of exit strategies and market caps, may not be the best strategy for an enterprise that is looking for sustainability and longevity over the long haul. An example of this refocusing on new outcomes can be found in the emergence of green economies, where new answers to issues of environmental sustainability and financial opportunity are forcing us to look differently at our traditionally desired strategies.

Recognizing emergent opportunities as they make themselves known rather than after the fact might be the difference between creating a revolutionary market shift and following a safer and more linear progressed change that may actually lead an enterprise toward a less successful outcome. But we can only realize such shift if we can develop and trust the skills to see what is about to emerge and then allow for the listening, reflection and conversations out of which these emergent opportunities can properly manifest.

# Engaged Emergence—Part 2

*Ed note: The second installment of Engaged Emergence was published a few months after the first. Rather than artificially combine them into one piece, we have chosen to run them as distinct, but related entries.*

Engaged Emergence is about the presence required to witness emergence as it is happening. More specifically, I have defined emergence as cause, condition, and effect. For those familiar with my particular Buddhist affliction—they say it should only last a lifetime or two—it might have been evident that the definition I used was also the common definition in Buddhist circles for Karma.

Karma is simply the effect that our actions create in the world we encounter. There is actually not too much here on the woo-woo-ometer that anyone would disagree with. What we do in the world, what we bring to each interaction, within a given environment, allows new things to emerge. What makes this connection between emergence and Karma interesting is that Karma isn't an event that just happens, it is a causal chain.

Within Karma, all our previous actions build on one another. Every actualization within our individual possibility space is carried with us into our next interaction, and they all influence the possibilities that make themselves known to us and their next iteration. We tend to think of emergent interactions as singular events—two or more agents interact and what can emerge is greater than the sum of the parts—rather than seeing it as two fully-developed causal chains interacting, with the history of both influencing what emerges. When looking at the process of the emergent event, we have to take into account that both agents bring all of this into each encounter. That's complexity.

Now for those long-time complexity arhats who have toiled and dallied in the world as it appears to show up, you may have thought in the back of your mind that delving into this soup of complex interactions would one day lead to enlightenment. Well, you just might be right.

In order to see emergence, as it emerges, requires presence. And to be present means that we aren't distracted by iPods, twitter, text messages, Netflix, the baseball playoffs or the looming deadline that is rapidly pressing down on us because we have been watching the baseball playoffs. It is about being mindful. Now mindfulness is not a spiritual or religious term, it is simply our ability to focus our mind on the landscape in front of us. Whenever we find ourselves distracted by the pheromones arising next to us, the blue, cloud-spotted skies out the window, or the piece of tape stuck to the top of the table, it is our ability to bring our minds back to our focus that we call mindfulness. When the alluring scent catches us and pulls us away from the landscape before us, we immediately become mind-filled and our original focus is lost.

Now I can hear the call arising, "well sometimes distraction is needed, and must be paid its due attention, especially when the olfactory nerve is so stimulated." And at that moment, it is our causal chain of experience that will ultimately determine if we follow that distraction, and then attempt to reapply our presence so that we might recognize what could be truly emerging from this new landscape, or return to our original focus.

It is at this instant, when the possible and actual are about to meet, that our ability to either recognize, or miss, the signposts telling us that something new and emergent is about to happen takes place. If we are present we see what is happening. If not, we miss it. Neither experience could have occurred independently of our causal chain of experience. However, we should be clear that Karma, like emergence, is not fate. Each of our possibility spaces is visible only to what we are able to see. How many of us have found ourselves in this position—that the possible was on the verge of actualizing and we didn't see what was actually emerging until after the fact? "Wow, I didn't see that coming." If we had only been present enough to read the signs correctly, rather than being distracted and completely mind-filled by other things, we might have seen what was taking place right in front of us.

Suffice it to say, to be fully conscious of the impact of our causal chain of emergent experiences on our next interaction, requires a level of Buddhahood most of us have yet to attain. However, our ability to recognize this notion of 'Engaged Emergence'—witnessing emergence as it is happening—can be developed through practice. Within this mindful practice, we are, in essence, influencing what we bring to the table. If we are simply building on our habitual causal chain of experience, we need to learn to change the pattern of the experiences. That is a learned operation and one that can be practiced. And like any such undertaking, whether it's learning to play a guitar without either Rock Band or Guitar Hero, or painting a pastoral landscape, our first attempts usually suck. But, if we continue to practice, we gain a level of mastery over that to which we are applying our focus.

In practicing this level of engagement, we discover that something rather unexpected happens. When we operate from a mindful image of the world we encounter, we see things we might previously have missed. We still bring our causal chain of experience with us, but as we break through the patterned behavior and habitual responses that have influenced it in the past, and add a new and more present way of looking at the world we encounter, the possibility space surrounding us enlarges and we see more within it with greater clarity, so that when something does appear that we hadn't seen before, we recognize it before it hits us on the side of the head or passes us by.

It is at every moment of interaction between two or more agents that the causal chain of experience of each agent surfaces and their individual thinking becomes biased by it. We tend to discount this, attempting to sanitize it out of the equation for the sake of simplicity, but we cannot do that. How or if we react is always based on the complex mix of our joined experiences, and unless we can do things differently that will break this pattern of reactive thinking, we will invariably miss the opportunity to see what new might emerge as it emerges. In some cases, this may not be as critical. We have been looking back at what has emerged for much of our lives, and often late getting to the party because of it. But now, when our ability to act quickly may be essential to moving forward success-fully, engaging in an interaction, with focused and mindful intent, aware of what we bring to the table, can be the difference between seeing the next great emergent oppor-tunity or becoming an also-ran.

We can redirect our causal chain of experience, our karma if you will, by acting differently and being more present when we do. The first step in this emergent process, however, is recognizing that it is influencing us before we can do anything really differently. As the Buddhists say, "Karma, neh?"

# Causal Clouds and Sudden Brainstorms

You and I interact and something emerges out of that interaction that is greater than the sum of our two parts. We might call that a simple emergent interaction. And that perception might be accepted as true except for one slight little addendum: to get to this point of connection, we both have led lives that have been anything but simple. Looking back, since we can only see this looking back, we bring to each moment in which we encounter another, our own personal causal chain of experience that informs, shapes and influences every next step we take. If you don't think that's a complex series of interactions, consider that it takes approximately 20,000 neuron interactions for a thought to emerge into consciousness and then think of all the thoughts that arise when you first meet that someone special. I guess love ain't so simple.

Like it or not, we operate within a vast array cloud of interactions with an equal array of nonlinear connections. Every thought we have, every organization we work with, every time we walk through a mall, this causal cloud forms and reforms our engagements with each other, as well as our making choices to avoid each other—for example, the homeless person you might have walked around this morning. Now there are some people who might refer to this as a vast network of interactions, and I admit, I was once one of those people. But it seems human interactions are not as neat as a network. As my friend and colleague Michael Lissack will tell you, what we are describing here is not so much a network, but an artwork. And true to that description, we could easily describe our encounters together as a creative and emergent process that reflects the world we see before us and the world we have experienced in the past.

If a linear network, with defined nodes and connections isn't what we've created, then perhaps we can co-opt the software visualization of a cloud to describe these collective interactions: a great nebulosity in which we find a vast number of shifting and interconnecting touch points of connection, and within which the conditions encountered influence every interaction. Ultimately, what emerges can produce a variety of outcomes and effects.

And so we go to work every day within this vast atmospheric space, in which we are constantly on the search to find more effective ways to improve how we can get our work done. And, more often than not, we end up with little bandwidth to sort through the complex patterns that coalesce from our interactions with coworkers, customers and suppliers. In doing so, we become even less effective in finding the crystallized emergent opportunities we might create together to operate more effectively. However, it is exactly this ability to share capacities that opens our bandwidth and is an essential aspect to our process of getting things done. The upshot is, if we're unable or unwilling to share, we can never expect to solve the complexity we encounter. Within this environment, collaboration becomes not just a tool, but the only means to surface new and novel solutions to the challenges that present themselves within any community.

But collaboration is not as simple a task as just being willing to share. We can't escape how we got to this moment. As mentioned above, each of us brings an entire life's worth of causal experience to each interaction. So when we then find ourselves within this cloud of causal touch points with our collaborators, we can't assume their experience is ours, nor can we anticipate how this amalgam of experience will affect what might emerge.

Within the emergent process, something new emerges because it has been afforded by something else, as a chair affords sitting. As we operate within the collaborative cloud of our causal interactions, the ability to afford our common and uncommon experience becomes of even greater importance. It does not take a great deal of reflection to remember a collaborative experience that failed because of someone's unwillingness to tolerate someone else within the group. So, when we create dysfunctional organizations and teams in which tolerance and understanding of others is far from what is encouraged, is it any wonder that the resulting storms rarely produce anything more than greater intolerance and few effective solutions?

Creating an atmosphere in which we can accommodate others is not a *nice-to-have* within the collaborative process, it is a must have. Because we can't help but create a great cloud of interaction in our collaborative encounters, we have to be aware of this if we want brainstorms, not destructive hurricanes.

So how do we effectively seed these brainstorms? It begins by establishing rapport, by sharing our stories and by understanding that we are interdependent complex adaptive systems that must find ways of working together or the larger complex system of which we are a part will either spit us out, kill us, or die itself. Think of how our own human body responds to invading viruses? Nature has no problem with any of these kinds of responses. We do, and therefore we must learn to act accordingly.

So, how do we avoid calamities like this? When we shift our perception of each other—how we see each other, our understanding of the models we might have created about each other—we must also shift the rules that we have put in place for ourselves that govern how we relate. If we shift our understanding but don't shift the rules that govern our behavior, nothing changes and nothing new will emerge.

The causal experience we bring into our collaborative efforts is neither preordained nor immutable. We can change and adapt. But we must also become conscious of how it informs our interactions with those with whom we interact, and we must be willing to let go of preconceived rules that might limit our ability to shift our behaviors to serve the greater good of the collaborative effort. Now this is not some message from Star Trek's Borg, where resistance to the collective is futile, but if we are entering the collaborative process holding onto the rules of our previous operations when the model has clearly changed, it is not only destructive to the process of sharing our capacity to solve shared challenges, it effectively eliminates our ability to adapt and survive. Bob Dylan reminded us that *A Hard Rain is Gonna Fall*, but we can avoid these kinds of cloudbursts if we begin to recognize that just like our colleagues, we bring a lifetime of causal experience to every swirling touch point we encounter. And while these experiences inform that moment, it doesn't need to precipitate an out-pouring that floods our capabilities to operate more effectively, together.

# Change, Change, Change—
## Change of Fools

I t's always the same ol' intransigent issues and the same ol' answers. So if we're really so smart, how come we're still up against a whole set of social systems and issues that are so out of control? Einstein has often been credited with saying, "The same level of thinking that caused a problem cannot be used to solve it." We're not all listening to Uncle Albie, are we?

About fifteen years ago, my colleague Howard Sherman introduced the notion of Principles, Models, Rules and Behaviors. It was a simple idea and one that he presented for the first time at a major conference, and took all of about twenty-minutes to do so. Howard, for those who knew him, was never one to beat around the bush about things he believed to be essential thinking. Now, nearly a decade after his passing, I keep returning to this description of the world, and marvel at both its prescience and its perception.

The notion was simple: Principles were ideas that because of their nature rarely if ever changed. Models were what we built to emulate the principle. Rules were those things we put in place to maintain the model, and behaviors were what we did to live the principles, based on the models we built and the rules that governed them.

Howard was always searching for a grand unifying theory of business and in many ways this perception of how the world operates was pretty damn close.

As we unpack this—Suppose, for example, we have a principle: "poor people always stay poor." Based on that notion we create social models that don't try and help poor people not be poor, but rather we try and find ways (and models) for applying a salve to ease the issue but not shift it. The rules we create for supporting organizations that service this issue and that also recognize the principle, however, well intended, by their design, restrict the behaviors that we as a society are willing to take to make this issue different.

The result is that no real change can ever happen. Nothing novel emerges from our inability to neither rethink a principle, nor shift the models based on that thinking.

But suppose we are capable of making a radical change in a principled position—and we can now say "Poor people don't have to remain poor." So we hurriedly begin reworking the models we've built and come up with a new set that describes our world based on the new principle we have established. However, in doing so, we forget to change the rules that govern that new model but support the old principle. The unfortunate result is that behaviors don't change and nothing new happens. But what gets blamed—our new principle was obviously wrong, because we still got more of the same.

This fight is being borne out in our political world on a daily basis. The fact that long after women have broken through the principles of our outdated sexual mores, we are trying to resurrect rules that will return behaviors to support a model of a principle that, by all rights, has never been valid.

It remains that if we cling to outdated principles—no matter how clever our models—we change nothing.

If we change our principles and our models, but still cling to old rules, our behaviors don't change, and we change nothing.

If we change our principles, models and behaviors, but keep our old rules in place, as had been the case with outmoded rules like the military's Don't Ask Don't Tell, where we were throwing people out of the military for acting according to new and accepted principles and models that went against old laws that had remained intact, nothing changes.

Intransigence seems to fall out of two of these precepts—our principles and the rules we put in place to make sure the principles stay principled.

A negative example of this is when we changed the rules and principles regulating banking. We created an incredible new set of models to support the new principle of deregulation and the un-ruled greedy behavior that followed crumbled economies around the world.

However, there can be a force for good. Enter the re-evolving space of collaboration. Complexicologists will recall such things as swarming and flocking. Neither of which has anything to do with hovering or nudging, (Ma, leave me alone!) which follow under a whole other realm of principles. Nonetheless, collaboration has been proving to be an effective means for not only shifting outdated principles, but the models, rules and behaviors that have kept them in place. Those of you with Jewish mothers know, even collaboration can't change some things.

With millions of dollars being spent on "change initiatives," and the incredible failure rate of these efforts, it's actually surprising that people haven't given up on this change thing altogether. Were it not for the obvious and continual change taking place around them, they probably would. Enter the company SecondMuse. Within the 'Muse's co-leadership team is Todd Khozein. Todd has joined and combined his divergent and eclectic experience as a trained Medical Doctor, an investment financial wizard, and a complexity Arhat. Now he's helped form a company dedicated to collaborative science and solving big problems through collaboration. But SecondMuse's process isn't just bringing groups of the best and brightest into the same space, which it does, but it's about being able to go through the innovation and change process in a completely different way that is experiential, practical, and ultimately creates successful change. It's about using the power and diversity of a collaborative interaction to surface something completely different, a new view of the world that requires new models be designed, new rules constructed and shifts behaviors to build the new model into something that really has an impact. Now in spite of this rather mechanical description of building and constructing, this is actually recognizing new combinations within the fluid space of collaboration.

SecondMuse has conducted these collaborative efforts to surface innovative solutions to global change, disaster issues and international development in the areas of Water, Energy, Health and soon Waste. With the diversity of software developers sitting next to physicists interacting with international development experts, aligned only by the common intention to further completely new ways of thinking, revolutionary innovations have emerged that can impact billions.

For example, the majority of people around the world still burn solid fuel to cook. Creating a cooker that can eliminate the carbon footprint of all those solid fuel emissions is only part of the equation. The principle is simple: the sustainability of the planet and its resources cannot withstand a growing population depleting those resources to feed itself and that in turn destroy the environment. An innovative model is presented: a solar cooker that totally reduces carbon emissions. But it's too expensive by a factor of 3. The cost puts it out of reach of all those who need it and who would change their depleting behaviors to use it.

Out of the discussion between these international development experts and product specialists, a software executive, who had invariably never developed anything but code, having listened to the interaction and trusted what he knew, recognized why the change was being stalled. There was a rule that needed to be changed that was holding up the whole process. The rule was that they must be paid for. The software exec proffered, however, what if these cookers didn't need to be bought, but could be leased at a fraction of the overall cost. That simple rule change made implementation possible.

Collaboration is about joining the experience and knowledge of everyone in the conversation and allowing that open source processing to take place within our very human condition. Out of that condition, we can surface what resides within the collective knowledge. However, none of it sticks unless and until we recognize that the capturing of an emergent property means that the new model we hold requires us to shift and perhaps throw-out the old rules that supported the former model, so that new behaviors can be freed to initiate the change that has emerged.

By recognizing what emerges from the cloud of collaborative interactions, impactful change can take place. But that discovery will remain nothing more than an idea until the simple perception Howard Sherman had about the profound relationship between our principles, models, rules and behaviors, and its impact on the implementation of something new and novel, is fully realized. Until then, even the development of the best cooker in the world will simply go up in smoke.

# Dissolving Cultural Intransigence

Within the realm of emergent phenomena, one of the most insidious combinations is prejudice and its fraternal twin, bigotry. Both arise out of the interaction between our fear and ignorance. Our inability to assimilate something being different than us or our experience of the world in which we live. Few of us are immune and many make a common practice out of it. And from that, our global society suffers under the further emergence of hatred, terror, and mistrust. It is a cycle that has continued since the dawn of what we call "consciousness."

It is "us" versus "them" in all its dastardly permutations and ramifications. And no one is the better for it. There are so many examples in the world today emerging from our fear-based interactions. From the streets of Ferguson, MO, to the killing waging in the Middle East, to our neighborlessness on our own city streets; if it ain't us, it's them.

I must admit, I only began thinking about this more closely when a recent request came to give some thought to the issues of Islamophobia. Wow, that got some things going for me.

I began doing some cursory research, and because there was a local Islamic center and mosque in my suburban LA neighborhood, a grand building on a hill a few blocks from my house, I decided I'd try and find someone there with whom to speak. I was surprised to find, although in hindsight it makes perfect sense, that there was no mention or reference online to the existence of this beautiful structure or what it housed. The closest listing was for an Islamic Center about 10 miles away. So, I called them.

Then, something rather extraordinary happened. I never spoke with anyone. But as I was listening to a recording of a very foreign sounding voice outlining upcoming events and prayer services, much of it spoken in a language I couldn't understand, I began feeling something arising in my body. It was distinct and it was obvious. It was fear.

Without warning, without cause, I felt the rapid rise of energy coursing through my body. It wasn't anticipation. It wasn't excitement. I was experiencing exactly what I was calling to learn more about. My journalistic distance and biases, always suspect, were now completely shattered. It was clear that in order to examine the issue, I didn't need to speak with an authority to confirm what Islamophobia looked like or how it showed-up. I needed to look at myself.

Many years ago, Walt Kelley and his famous cartoon character, Pogo, once said, "We have met the enemy and it is us." If just like me, others have these same feelings, then it seems pretty obvious that a deeper and more personal examination is required.

There is little question that the complexity of this problem is enormous. The deep seeded fear that emerges when we interact with "the stranger" is not only the stuff of novels and dreams, it fills our movies and TV screens. It's shouted out by 24-hour pundits and bloggers.

Was that always the case? Was there ever a time when the stranger was welcomed. A dear friend pointed to evidence of this with the Mork and Mindy show—of course, this stranger was white and Robin Williams in all his fullness. And even though he played an alien, he was not so foreign that we couldn't laugh along with his innocence of our culture.

There was also a time, a much younger time, when my openness to new friends, my curiosity about others was simply a part of my discovering the world around me, unprejudiced, unbiased by any outside influence. But things have changed in the world. The darkness and fear of that which is different permeates our media. Children have to be taught "stranger danger" as a normal part of growing up. Of course, as we interact with that barrage of stranger-fear, what emerges, what arises out of the muck, is even more fear. The curiosity that might allow us to view these situations differently is lost. Instead we are on-guard, reinforced, and entrenched. The unfortunate consequence of this security surfeit is a societal freeze, cultural intransigence.

Classically, the phase transition from ice to water to gas has helped folks visualize the distinctions between order, complexity and chaos. In terms of this discussion, when the conversation and attitudes are frozen, nothing fresh emerges. It is only after the thaw, within the watery pool of complexity, where the elements can move freely still within a bounded space, that any innovative interactions take place. This is the spawning pond, out of which something new and novel can emerge.

Cultural intransigence is that frozen state. Finding the solvent to dissolve both our personal and cultural solidity, and then translating that to a world stained by intransigence, is the challenge of this age. But how do we transform cultural fear without creating more and future aggression?

In the most recent report of the Organization for Islamic Cooperation's (OIC) publication, *Observatory*, covering October 2012 to September 2013, there is documentation of incidents in 18 nations involving attacks on mosques, desecration of Muslim graves, political and social campaigns against Islam and Muslims, intolerance directed against Islam and its sacred symbols, discrimination against Muslims in educational institutions, workplaces and airports, and other related phenomena.

As Richard Reoch, a former senior executive at Amnesty International explained it: "These incidents not only target Islam. They are part of a larger and deeply disturbing tendency worldwide to denigrate, demonize and unleash assaults, often with extreme cruelty, on entire groups of people, victimizing them for their identity. Like all forms of religious, ethnic or cultural hatred, what is happening is a direct threat to the principles of coexistence that are essential if people of different faiths and traditions are to live and flourish together.

I believe a deep-seated approach is needed to understand and heal what is happening across the globe. It will not end simply by denouncing it and seeking to suppress it. It will continue to burn. If there is to be an effective international roadmap for constructive action, it needs to be grounded in a far more profound dialogue, based on the enduring, noble and transcendent values of our respective traditions."

Creating such opportunities may seem unimaginable, but our failure of imagination is simply our inability to see beyond our own fear and trepidation. Since its inception, this column has been called *Adjacent Opportunities*, openly stolen from Philip Kauffman's *adjacent possible*.

The notion is that the adjacent opportunity is just one step away, but doesn't emerge and become available until we have taken the step before it.

Nothing is closer than an adjacency and we live in an adjacent world. This is why we can't allow our perception of separateness to prevail. But just like me, it arises.

The answer is often, "let us build bridges between." But the separation isn't that vast. It's just one step away. It's not necessary to transit this divide by leaping over a vast chasm, but rather by unceasingly engaging the adjacent interaction, having the dialogue, and deepening it by capturing each successive new opportunity we make, and moving forward from that point.

The simplicity of one step is deceptive. With every new step comes the possibility of a new understanding, which when internalized opens up the next, new opportunity.

What our experience shows us is the impossible and inconceivable become manifest whenever we willingly dissolve our frozen thinking, allow for new combinations to occur, and keep from refreezing what emerges. Shifting cultural intransigence is neither impossible nor inconceivable. It requires fearlessness and curiosity to welcome the stranger and create community. It also means not only recognizing our own fear, but the fear of the stranger, as well.

Our differences are our own making. Solidifying them is our own doing. Unmaking and dissolving them begins with each successive step forward. I realize, now, I need to take those steps, too. Can we walk together?

# Present Possible, Adjacent Possible, Possibly Possible

Everything feels so intransigent now, so solid, so desperate. The possibility for change not only feels like a distant possibility, it feels like things might never change. Is it possible to make it different? Are we stuck with the social ills plaguing us? While the options available and presented in this journal are often well-reasoned, highly intelligent and breathlessly notated, the solution I am about to provide here, may be one you couldn't imagine finding in an academic periodical. But then, it might just be that failure of imagination is the key to the strong box of our stuck-ness. Shifting intransigent thinking and taking new action about the social issues we find so frozen in place (the job, by the way of the social entrepreneurs in our midst), is not just about the solidity of our thinking, but perhaps also the encasement of our hearts. Let me offer this scenario that is not as crazy and touchy-feely as it might sound. So all you hardcore thinkers, let it go for just a moment. You'll feel more comfortable in a minute.

I open my heart to the world because it is possible, now. An adjacent possibility emerges for me to interact with another and share my open heart and their heart opens, too. And then, as we continue to interact with our open hearts toward others, it becomes possibly possible to open the hearts of billions around the world.

In this current world seemingly so filled with intolerance and aggression, something needs to be done to melt the solidity that characterizes our intransigent positions. In 1997, I co-wrote a book with the late and brilliant, Howard

Sherman, called *Open Boundaries*. In it, I offered a model called *A Sustainable Model for Inconceivable Development*, that was all about what was presently possible, shifting the adjacent possible, and bringing about the possibly possible.

Shortly after that book was published by Perseus Books, and with an appropriate amount of audacity, I sent a copy to our then US Secretary of Energy, and my former Congressman, Bill Richardson. I asked him to forward a second copy of *Open Boundaries* I had included, with the *Sustainable Model for Inconceivable Development* duly highlighted, to former Senator George Mitchell who was about to negotiate a peace settlement in Northern Ireland. Secretary Richardson, later Governor of New Mexico, wrote back to me that he had done as I had asked. Bill really is a good guy.

Now, I am not so audacious as to suggest that Senator Mitchell read the highlighted portion of the book he had received and employed my *Sustainable Model for Inconceivable Development* to find peace in Northern Ireland, but the possibility is possible, and there is no arguing with the fact that peace was attained. So, the only logical conclusion I, and possibly we, can ascertain from this is that it is possible to shift and melt the solidity of those things we have become so adept at creating and encasing.

So it begins. Open your heart, share your open heart with another, and together we can shift the world. Afraid to open your heart? Perhaps you think it's safer to live in a dangerous world filled with fear and hatred? Terrified by what might happen if you opened your heart and you were rejected? Well those are all good reasons for continuing our lemming-led march over the cliff to our self-destruction, aren't they? "I had to let our demise happen because I was afraid that by opening my heart to the world I might be laughed at, ridiculed, or worse yet, rejected by someone unable to open theirs."

Well, have no fear, SMID is here (OK, I won't use this acronym again)—and yes, it is an intellectual model that will take you step by step to a more open heart, and who knows, possibly peace in our lifetime.

When emergence happens, and we realize that things are not the same as we had previously thought, we are, in essence, changing our understanding of our system and the models we have devised to describe that system. It means that if we really want to realize change, we must adjust our behaviors and relationships according to our new understanding as well as the rules we have created to maintain that understanding of our system. So *The Sustainable Model for Inconceivable Development* starts by:

**Step 1:** Adjusting our models on the basis of the new understanding that has emerged.

**Step 2:** Adjust our relationships, our behavior and rules, according to our new understanding of our model.

**Step 3:** When we do this something new emerges, because something different always happens whenever there is an interaction between our models and behaviors, once we have taken the first two steps.

**Step 4:** Return to Step 1—go back and readjust our models on the basis of this new emergence.

**Step 5:** Return to Step 2—adjust our relationships on the basis of our new model.

**Step 6:** Return to Step 3—emergence happens within the interaction.

**Step 7:** Return to Step 1—we return to our models, adjusting them according to our new understanding.

**Step 8:** Return to Step 2—we adjust our relationships again.

**Step 9:** Return to Step 3—emergence happens.

**Step 10:** Return to Step 1—the process continues.

OK, you say, this is logical enough and satisfies the intellect, but what's all this heart stuff got to do with this? Perhaps, a little fictional story:

**Step 1:** I am introduced to a fellow at a coffee shop where I am a regular. He is about 180 degrees opposite from me in political, social and religious beliefs—OK we'll call this person a Republican. If I meet him as one of *them*, with all my preconceived notions of who *they* are, nothing changes and the world remains solid. However, if I meet him and I decide to open my heart to him, and in our conversation I find that even though his beliefs are completely differently from mine, he doesn't like seeing homeless people suffering on the streets, I hear something we share in common, and my feeling about this person shifts slightly.

**Step 2:** I go about my day, but I begin adjusting my opinion about him and how he shows up in the world.

**Step 3:** The next day we meet again at the coffee store, and I ask him what he thinks he could do to help a home-less person rather than just give them food or money? The response is, "well, we could give them a job." Suddenly, we're talking about my world. We sit down with our coffee, and begin talking about what giving "them" a job looks like. What if it weren't just a job? What would it look like if we helped people in this population start businesses—what would that entail? Suddenly, on the napkin in front of us, a plan starts to form.

**Step 4:** I head off for work, and I'm thinking, "What was that?" My thinking about this person begins to shift again as possibilities start to emerge.

**Step 5:** The next day over coffee, he has already found a table for us, and the first question about my family is asked and I ask about his. We both have girls. We laugh. Both hearts open a little further.

**Step 6:** We look again at our ideas from the day before, but there's an enthusiasm about them now that feels different. It's just notes on a napkin, but we agree that a curriculum that teaches basic business tenants would be required and teaching it couldn't be rushed—we would need mentors to work with each person to help them in areas in which they had no experience. I mention a business professor I know who could help.

**Step 7:** A good part of the rest of my day is thinking about this other person who has suddenly taken up my mornings and with whom, we seem to be doing... I'm not sure what, but we are doing. The beliefs that are held by us about the world are not important to this or to us doing this together.

**Step 8:** The next morning we have both invited others to join us. My business professor friend is there as is the head of his church's outreach group, with whom my colleague is friends.

**Step 9:** A population of homeless people with whom, it turns out, the university and the church have been working is identified. The professor can bring in some students to act as mentors and the church offers its community room to hold classes to begin a joint homeless entrepreneurs' education program. There is great enthusiasm and joy. We all shake hands, laugh and embrace with hearts open at what is possible before us.

**Step 10:** The process continues and within a month, the first population of homeless entrepreneurs begins their training. And the process continues…

When adjustments are made after each emergent possibility arises, what we see after the second or third level of emergence is a development that would have been absolutely inconceivable from the perspective of our initial understanding. Our tendency, however, is to stop the process after the first or second level of emergence and close the system back down to protect the initial, fabulous innovation that has come about.

The key to sustaining the development process is the continual adjustment of our models, behaviors and the rules we establish to guide our relationships. As soon as we freeze the model, and, subsequently, our relationship to our behaviors, we return to orthodox novelty— the same "stuckness" with which we began. Emergent novelty—real innovation—is possible only when the system is open to what is presently possible and adjacently possible. And then it is in the realm of the possibly possible that what was once inconceivable becomes actualized and we can have peace in Northern Ireland… or perhaps Democrats and Republicans working together.

When we fear there isn't time to allow complex interactions and emergence to happen, we need to address more closely the work unleashed by the previous emergence and the rules we have created to support our models. What has previously emerged fertilizes the ground for the next emergence that will invariably arise, but if we are still holding onto old rules that no longer support what has emerged, there is no room for change and we once again solidify where we are and refuse to do anything differently.

OK, now let's get back to the heart of the matter, here. When all our lives are being adversely affected by the intransigence we impose when we close our minds to what is possible, doesn't it make sense to change that and start opening our hearts? The love and compassion we create as human beings is not insignificant when addressing the issues surrounding us. There is a modern example of this that took place in South Africa. Had the majority population been prompted to act against the oppressors who had defiled them for decades, there would have been a bloodbath like few the world had seen. But they did not. Led by Nelson Mandela and Desmond Tutu, they chose to come from the heart, and provided the world with a novel new model, truth and forgiveness (reconciliation). Their decision to come from their hearts rather than unleash the ravages of hatred was one of the greatest events of the 20th century. It was an example for the 21st century of what can emerge when the heart is chosen over the intransigence of how things are normally done. The new leaders of South Africa recognized this novel emergent possibility before them and then took the steps necessary to assure their countrymen not to embed themselves so solidly in their old models that they sank everything rather than do something that could benefit everyone. It took courage and leadership—"courage" comes from the French *courage—coming from the heart*. They shattered the model, adjusted their behaviors and rules accordingly and what emerged was something that was inconceivable in the eyes of the world.

It can happen. We're just one step away from that adjacent possibility. I say, let's open our hearts and take it!

# Mindful Complexity

The opposite of being mindful is being mind-filled. In a state of mind-filledness there is no room for anything new to enter. The paradoxical response to this condition is often to distract yourself even more, with music, food, movies, web-surfing and all sorts of other discursive activities. When looked at from this perspective, you would think that this additional informational input would only acerbate the condition...and guess what, it does. The more distractions you input into your mind, the less mindful you are and the more mind-filled you become. I would think that at this point it would be fairly obvious why one might experience overload?

Within today's complex work environments, as well as simply staying abreast of what's going on in the world around us, we make a choice every moment—be here or go there. And overwhelmingly we choose to go there.

Don't believe me? Try for yourselves. Try to sit still for five minutes without distracting yourself with something else. That includes telling yourself a story, making lists about what you have to accomplish, what you need at the store, how many cracks there are on the floor, what sports event you want to watch, taking the wash out of the dryer—no entertainment. OK that last one isn't very entertaining, but it could be especially if you're trying to be aware of all your other distractions. Even reading this piece is a means of distraction... but don't stop reading, yet.

So why should you care if you are mind-filled or mindful? Let's take your ability to pick up cues within the environment in which you are operating. Cues are those elements that point in the direction of something new about to emerge. They can show up as physical evidence, a sensation or an intuitive awareness, an expectant feeling you might get walking into a crowded room. If your mind were filled, any new information that might emerge would probably not register as more than background noise.

Now, let's extend that notion of picking up cues as the precursor to actually recognizing something emerge, as it emerges, rather than trying to track it down after the fact amid all the muddle and debris. This is something akin to trying to figure-out a whodunit mystery in real time. Miss a cue and the mystery remains unsolved. If you aren't able to be present enough to see and feel the environment with a mind not filled by other distractions and junk, you'll invariably be surprised when you discover it was Professor Plum in the conservatory with the iPad. Oh, that's who did it!—after the fact.

In a business context, this is the ability to be moving toward recognizing an innovative idea rather than looking back and trying to figure out what just happened. If others are busily looking back and you're moving forward, who is ahead of the game?

The ability to become more mindful and make space in your mind allows another profound occurrence to take place. The more you practice mindfulness, the less you become fixated on your own ideas, locked-in by your own biases. Being free from fixed ideas allows you to be more comfortable sitting with a blank canvas. This is the open space upon which the opportunity for real innovation, something truly new and now, can emerge.

Mindfulness is not something that is simply learned and once learned, you've got it. It is a practice and requires practice. One well-known technique for developing mindfulness is meditation; the act of stabilizing the mind. This is not about learning to stop your thinking, as some mistakenly purport. Rather it is about being able to watch your thoughts without holding on to any of them.

One metaphor describing the relationship between meditation and thought is that you are a mountain and your thoughts are like clouds floating by. You have no means to jump on one of the clouds or pack it away for later. It just moves on by.

Once you have received initial instruction in how to meditate, something that has been passed down person to person for millennia, it takes practice to begin letting go of the clutter that has been amassed. Mind-filled hording is no less an issue than hording material stuff in your own home. But, by learning to clear some of that out, you actually discover you've created more space. And by being able to sit within that space and not freak out because you've gotten rid of the comfort of the clutter, something rather remarkable begins to take place. Clarity begins to emerge. And when you can be comfortable simply sitting in the space of your mind while interacting with others, a variety of things can transpire. One, crucial to this discussion, is that when something emerges out of that interaction with others, it becomes evident to you and not lost amid the stacks of old New Yorkers you've carefully stored in the corner.

This ability to cue-spot and capture what emerges within a collaborative interaction actually requires more than just a mindful space. There are six steps within this process.

1. Mindfulness—the ability to return focus to the topic at hand without clinging to thoughts;

2. Awareness—the ability to recognize that you have been pulled away from the interaction;

3. Listening—the ability to hear what is being said within all segments of the environment—inner-personal and intra-personal;

4. Offering—the ability to trust what is known and to capture and present what has emerged;

5. Furthering—the ability to reapply what has emerged to deepen the conversation and afford the next level of emergence, and;

6. Discovery—the ability to identify novelty as it emerges.

Being able to capture the innovative moment, however, begins with mindfulness. It takes a willingness to not be stuck in your fixed ideas about the world you encounter. Modeling that behavior as a leader makes it OK for others to do so as well. The result is that it can bring an enterprise to the front of the pack both from an innovative perspective and from being the kind of place people want to work. This is not a management technique. This is leadership.

# Resilient Elasticity

'd really like to think it's all about me, and most days, I probably do think just that. But I find that I tend to wake-up the next morning after a totally me-day feeling something is inherently missing. While some of us may run from the fact, we are relational and social beings. We interact with each other and learn, grow and develop from what emerges out of those interactions. Sometimes those encounters are innovative, exciting and expansive. Others not so much.

When we characterize challenging encounters, words and phrases arise like blow-up, exploded, went ballistic, burst my bubble, erupted, shattered, broke-up, flooded, blew a gasket and then I blew my top. All of these describe and explain how we've somehow exceeded the capacity of our boundaries and they couldn't handle the strain and crumbled.

In the world of emotional intelligence, we speak about the quality of resilience as being a critical factor in our emotional style. It is often described as our ability to recover from an unexpected turn of events. If we're very resilient we recover quickly. If not, the experience was undoubtedly accompanied by one of the aforementioned words or expressions. Our boundaries had lost their elasticity and couldn't contain the emotion that arose, so they simply burst asunder.

Recovering from that kind of experience is usually not so quick because it means we have to figure out how we're going to rebuild our breached boundaries. That reconstruction, while not always involving a lot of moving parts, often requires some form of forgiveness coming from at least one of the participants involved. And forgiveness or having to ask for forgiveness can be very trying to some.

There is another approach which is much less painful and shame-filled, and ultimately far more satisfying: Accommodation. Accommodation requires us to take a good look at every inch of the boundaries we've created for ourselves and find where we have solidified, rigid, and unyielding segments that when tightened even further become frail and brittle.

In relational terms, accommodation is really about being able to make room for the other without busting a gut, or exceeding our boundaries. It's the supple flexibility to move with whatever shows up. It's that elasticity which is a hallmark of our resilience, but it signals something more. It is a demonstration of our ability to be at ease with the world we encounter.

In the complex world of interactions and emergence, distractions and *busyness*, it is easy to become overloaded and overwhelmed. The feeling that courses through our bodies when that "too much" sensation cascades from our shoulders down into the pit of the stomach is a real-time emotionometer. Those of us who recognize that indicator sounding its physical alarm can fend off the emotional outburst that can arise fueled by just one more proverbial straw. That moment when we can stretch our tolerance by just the merest of an iota, feel the feeling and then relax with it, is accommodation in action.

What powers our inability to accommodate is our need to be right, because after all it is all about me. I was recently in northern California, a few miles from the devastating Valley fire, burning through 100 square miles of terrain and charring over 500 homes. The wine valley communities of Calistoga, Napa, *et al.*, opened their doors, wallets, and hearts to the families that lost everything they had in the firestorm that consumed their everything.

Those living within the vineyards immediately did all they could to accommodate those whose homes, livestock and personal boundaries had perished in the smoke. It wasn't about who was right, who gave the most, it was about their ability to meet and accommodate the Other, so that perhaps their recovery might be just that much easier.

It's interesting that what I heard again and again after the devastation had taken its toll, was "the important thing is we're all alive and people have been so generous." We can accommodate even ruin when we are touched by the example of another's willingness to reach out toward us.

What is missing in all of this is that it doesn't have to take a crisis for us to accommodate each other, to be more malleable, lithe, bendable in the face of another's human-ness.

I once was told a definition of anger that has resonated with me time and again, probably because I continually fall prey to it. "Anger is when someone doesn't follow the script you've written for them." Accommodation is the recognition that we all have our own scripts, and none of us are sure of our lines or the next action we're expected to take. Of course for some of us, the really hard part about accommodating your script is one's eagerness in wanting to rewrite it.

Accommodating your script means I have to be willing to rewrite my own. This may sound like Hollywood heresy, but it's amazing what we can accomplish together if we are willing to do so. What nature shows us again and again, is that it's really not all about me. And if we are courageous enough to let go of me, for even the briefest of times, the world doesn't swallow us up. It embraces us, welcomes us, and accommodates us, as well.

Now if this sounds too soft and squishy, check it out for yourself the next time a co-worker, a friend or a loved one blows it, and you don't let it grab you. How does that change the dynamic of that interaction, and then the next one?

The political world may think it's OK to not accommodate the other, but the natural world will ultimately win out.

## Well-Being to Well-Doing

What does well-being feel like? Perhaps a little like this. We're sitting at Cole's Coffee on a sunny Sunday morning in Berkeley, CA. The tables are alive with conversation and laughter. The bright sky fills the air with a pale blue beauty that speaks unending opportunity and possibility. At least, that's how it feels. My wife and I are connecting with our dear friend, Stephen Heffernan, a former business partner and a long-time colleague. It's a perfect day to be sitting out at the sidewalk tables and sharing updates, good coffee and our long-standing friendship. Satisfied, content and engaged. Isn't that what well-being is supposed to feel like?

I talk about the work I'm doing around meditation, mindfulness and well-being. Work Stephen and I have discussed on many occasions. But this time Stephen says, without hesitation, "As long as well-being leads to well-doing."

Well, of course it does. Now let me immediately be clear about this—we are not talking about the notion of doing well, which can certainly be a part of well-doing. But doing well is much more about how my doing benefits me, rather than how it benefits others.

After a little research, it was clear that there were a lot of references to the idea that well-doing was about the right actions we take that benefit others. There were also statements that well-doing could equally refer to how we implement and accomplish programs and projects. I have no problem with that perspective as another piece of the puzzle, but I think when we couple well-doing with well-being, there's an opportunity that emerges that is even greater than accomplishment.

I confessed to Stephen shortly after our initial conversation that my plan was to steal his observation about the relationship between these two aspects of wellness and write about them in connection to my work. As a consultant, he graciously offered me his bill with a smile.

I had mentioned to him that I had been gathering a great deal of research about the science of well-being from Dr. Richard (Richie) J. Davidson, and his remarkable book, *The Emotional Life of Your Brain,* written with Sharon Begley. In it, Davidson documents his findings and years of scientific research into why, where and how the brain acts as it does, as well as how and why we respond and react as we do to our emotions. As founder of the Center for Investigating Healthy Minds at the University of Wisconsin, Madison, Davidson describes how a true sense of well-being can and does affect how we relate to the world that arrives before us.

The healthier and more pronounced our feelings of well-being are, the greater resilience we can muster and then exhibit when something unexpected arises. Resilience, in this instance, is our ability to recover quickly. But I think it also extends to our ability to accommodate others. From the standpoint of well-doing, accommodating others is a critical differentiation from doing just for me. Our ability to accommodate and rebound quickly also helps us maintain a more positive outlook on life and be healthier for it.

From my perspective, it is out of this sense of the goodness of life that we find ourselves both willing and wanting to share that goodness with others. Generosity and accommodation are a natural extension, which not too surprisingly leads to an increased sense of happiness and well-being.

Now, I want to be clear, we're not talking about a temporary happiness, or a momentary feeling of elation, but a lasting sense of well-being that serves us in all situations that show-up. It is from this place of personal health and wellness, both physically and mentally, that we can begin to see there are others who are not as *well* as we are.

For me, this is the point when well-being leads to well-doing. I would be interested to know if it were possible to truly realize a personal sense of well-being and then not care about anyone else's. I want to believe that our brains couldn't function that way. I think it is part of our innate being that when we are within a place of deep satisfaction and well-being that the needs of others can't be ignored.

One rather remarkable example is Grant Perry. Grant's life was one of tremendous accomplishment and amazing possibility. That is until a rare form of cancer put him and his family through a spiral of seemingly endless treatments and operations. But Grant made it through these excruciating procedures, and rather than simply doing what he had to do to survive, only for himself, he realized that others might also have to endure the painful path he has had to follow. From that realization, he developed an app called *Patient Pilot*, to empower patients and guide them as they navigate through the maze of treatments so they can return to at least a semblance of well-being.

As Grant explains, "My main goal is to help people take control of their well-being." He describes a doctor's visit at a famous clinic in which everyone is functioning under the pressure and time constraints of the medical system they are a part of. In a situation like this, patients are reluctant to ask questions. Doctors also feel the system simply doesn't afford them the time they would like with every patient. "As I was going through my own experience," Grant offers, "and I was fairly sophisticated, there were still questions I didn't ask. Lingo in the pathology I didn't understand. And the doctor didn't explain it. I didn't even know what choices I had."

But it was an experience Grant had while in an examination room waiting to see a doctor at Yale University that moved him to act. He over-heard the doctor telling another patient about a surgery Grant had previously had. The doctor briefly described the procedure. What he failed to describe, Grant knew, was any of the discomfort the patient would feel, or that one couldn't talk after the surgery, or his own recollections of feeling incredibly helpless. He also noted that the patient wasn't asking any questions, partly, he conjectured, because this was a very busy and important doctor at Yale. "So, I began thinking," he told me from his home in Washington, DC, "What could be done to help people like that?"

His first inclination was a sign that could be placed in every doctor's office, "If you don't know what's happening next, ask! Do you understand? If not, don't leave the office until you do."

Since people don't always know what to ask, Grant set out to develop his app that would prompt the right questions throughout the process and in doing so empower the patient and also serve the doctor.

I'm always inspired by folks who are motivated to move beyond themselves and genuinely help others, many of whom they may never know. I was having a discussion with Grant's father-in-law about the messages we have sent far out into space toward other planetary systems to describe our human life. According to Grant's father-in-law, one word many scientists liked was, altruistic. But for me, that was too individually based. I think we are far more interdependent, far more reliant on each other than we might normally imagine. So, for me, the word was relationship. Everything we do as a biological system is some kind of relationship, some healthier than others. But for a relationship to be at its most functional and healthiest requires a level of well-being that propels us to reach out toward the other and connect. It is at this intersection with the other where well-doing emerges. And when we do it right, it feels just like that feeling of well-being.

# The Resilience of Mindfulness—
## From Fear-based Leadership to
## Courageous Compassion

Like many of us involved in creating good work that is purposefully of benefit to others, I have spent the last 20 odd years (some of them being very odd) practicing mindfulness. And while this term has gotten a great deal of attention lately with everyone, including the business world, clambering to undertake whatever activity they can to access it, there has always been something missing for me. Not from the practice but from my understanding of the practice.

What I didn't realize, even though I'm sure it has been said again and again, is that mindfulness equals heartfulness. When I finally heard this expressed, it made perfect sense to me. I get heartfulness. I get being open-hearted and compassionate. I get that it took my practice of mindfulness to lead me back to my heart. Even though I've been told there is no separation between mind and heart, I had to live it. Like mindfulness, heartfulness requires courage. The French word for courage essentially means from the heart. And to recognize and act from one's heartfulness, we must be willing, vulnerable and courageous.

There are so many forces out there, especially in the business world, so terrified of the power of heartfulness that they will do all they can to squash it. For example, those who blanch at using the "L" word in the workplace, believing it something akin to rattling off a string of expletives in church. Or thinking it's safer to be indifferent to an employee going through a difficult time personally rather than applying a little gentleness and kindness.

It must have been that at some point along their non-courageous path, these folks reasoned you couldn't be ruthless if you were heartful. And they are right. You can't. As scary as ruthlessness can be, it doesn't take any courage to act against the interests of others. However, being compassionate for others does. You have to be willing to open your heart, fearlessly welcome others in and not shy away from the feeling. There is nothing wrong in coming from this place and it belongs everywhere. What greater entrepreneurial asset could there be than compassion and courage?

I just attended a weekend-long session called "Being Brave," that featured Shambhala's Sakyong Mipham Rinpoche, Ani Pema Chodren and the Episcopal Bishop of California, Mark Andrus. During the event, the 1,500 assembled were directed into affinity group sessions that encircled the expansive and spacious Craneway Pavilion in Richmond, CA, where the event was held. I was one of the hosts within the Economics and Business affinity area, and it was jammed with folks eager to shift the fear-based and ruthless business world paradigm to one that was more humane and related.

They weren't waiting for permission. These were entre-preneurs and business people who were doing it already. They felt the heartful connection among their compatriots, but they questioned whether it was possible to shift a business culture so enshrined in what they perceived as greed and aggression.

But, "they" are not the enemy. The courageous perspective is not one of disillusionment, disappointment or frustration with "them." Like mindfulness, heartfulness is about recognizing that just like me, they are also disillusioned, disappointed and frustrated. Feeling that way toward them creates a gulf that is even greater between us.

Courage is our ability to meet mind-to-mind and heart to heart. The mounting evidence, of course, points to the fact that businesses that recognize this are out-performing their competitors. But that doesn't stop those who have stuck their heads so deep in the sand they've got no room for breath let alone to feel their hearts.

They are afraid, and that fear drives their activities against rather than with. But, we are rapidly discovering, as one ardent eco-climatist pointed out to me, that those against will suffer just as much as those operating with.

If rampaging tornedos and devastating hurricanes don't scare people into changing, we need a new way to approach this. Fighting fear with more fear is like pouring gas on a fire. This isn't a time for greater combustion. So what would happen if we used compassion and courage to calm fear instead? It has worked before. The names Gandhi, Mandela, Tutu, Aung San Suu Kyi, and King come to mind for instance. The greatest social transitions made in the past two centuries have all come about when compassion and courage were applied to calm and over-come fear. And yet, we forget.

We love our kittens. We love our puppies. We love our mothers. We love our children. We even love our country. We don't quite know how to love each other. One would think that the notion of being heartful would transcend religious intransigence. Heartfulness is certainly preached in every religious institution that embraces sacred words. It seems to be the common ground for all of us no matter what we believe.

As people tied by our social interdependence, what keeps us from living that in our workplaces, governments and our relationships with our neighbors? Fear? Mistrust? Differences? The only way we can surmount fear, mistrust and the diversity we don't understand is with courage. And courage arises from the heart, from our compassion for each other, from our willingness to meet. Truly meet.

That conversation begins between you and me. In having that conversation, together, heart to heart, mind to mind, we can affect the changes we want to see. Ingrained fear does not fall in a day. But ingrained compassion and courage can be both persistent and patient. Being mindful is being heartful. Now, extend that out.

# Rugged Collaborationism

What would compel someone like David Haskell to lead an organization that is willing to go into the most dangerous places on earth to see to the needs of those trapped in those locations? What drives a woman like Karen Tse to end torture in 32 nations by training local public defenders to uphold the humanity of those accused? What inspired Bart Weetjens to even think he could train giant rats to sniff out land mines in Africa and then accomplish this task saving thousands of lives threatened by this treachery? Why do social innovators do this work?

In cases like these, there is great darkness across the lands in which these social entrepreneurs work, but the good news is they often cast a very bright light into the recesses of the worlds they encounter. So, what is it that informs their values, motivation, and inspiration? I was recently given a small book in which I found just such a principle and along with it many of the reasons why we social entrepreneurs do the work we do. The book: The Shambhala Principle (Harmony, 2013).

At its core, The Shambhala Principle is the basic goodness inherent in everyone living on this planet. This Principle of basic goodness sounds pretty simple, but it is the cornerstone for creating a good human society. It's why social entrepreneurs can venture courageously into the darkness. They also know they cannot endeavor to shift what seems like intractable social challenges, alone. Desmond Tutu reminded us of this when he shared his story of feeling like a light bulb. When the lamp can be turned on, the bulb illuminates everything in its path. But if the light bulb is unscrewed and laid next to the lamp, no matter how hard it might try, it is unable to shine. The point being, we don't and can't do this work alone. Our ability to bring light into hidden places requires all of us to work together.

It requires a society. The Shambhala Principle, as articulated by its author and the leader of the Shambhala Buddhist lineage, the Sakyong Mipham Rinpoche, is about creating a society that understands and acts upon our relationship to each other and to the world we encounter. This is not a religious offering in any sense of the word. It's purely a human understanding of what it takes to awaken our interconnectedness.

What separates those driven to find social innovation from those challenging old models in the business world? Not much when you understand that both activities are essentially based on relationships. And, as The Shambhala Principle makes clear, the success of these innovative approaches is only as great as the innovator's ability to relate to others.

In The Shambhala Principle, it begins with "just you and me." To some this may seem like a radical shift from the cultural perspective of the "rugged individualist." But this now-failed principle, brought to us in the $17^{th}$ century by John Locke and his compatriots, no longer holds up in the $21^{st}$ century. Now, to effectively get anything done, we need to see ourselves as rugged collaborationists, engaged with each other in building a healthy and prosperous society.

As the Sakyong describes it: "In a society where the individual is exalted, it is harder to tune into 'you' because we are so involved with 'me.' This isolationist policy makes it difficult to grow. Conversations become a one-way street instead of a two-way rapport."

"On the other hand, in a society of 'just you and me,' encounters become a way of celebrating our humanity because when we all contribute freshness and flexibility to the one-to-one ceremony, our growth is exponential. Kindness and wisdom are displayed in many directions. Ideas cross-pollinate, new theories arise. From this self-invigoration, we create art, poetry, and literature, as well as science and engineering. Let us now re-empower the word society so that every time we have a conversation, it is an expression of possibility."

This expression of the possible only arises when we have the conversation. This is true in the world of business innovation and social innovation. Our interactions with each other produce a whole new realm of "adjacent opportunities," opportunities that are just one step away from where we are right now, but which didn't exist until we took the step before. This is the basis of our ability to change, to affect change, and of our system to accommodate change.

Change begins with the meeting, with the conversation. So when social entrepreneurs venture into places of danger or darkness, they turn on the light with a conversation between "just you and me." What emerges from that moment of human interaction may seem magical, but it is actually very ordinary magic, at best. Especially if you define magic as a transformation by the unexpected.

But this simple act of talking with each other can melt cultural intransigence within even the most entrenched social systems. It means "talking with," not "talking to you," which of course implies, "listening with." The answer is not in me or you, but in you and me—rugged collaborationism.

It is imperative for those of us who call ourselves Social Entrepreneurs to learn that making change doesn't start with a grandiose scheme of us helping them. It begins with a single interaction between us, followed by another, and then another and in this continuum of interaction lives change. It is not a soliloquy, or a rage against the storm, but a recognition of the basic goodness each of us operates from and which can be touched with a simple reaching out to another. Change begins here.

When I asked 24 chapter contributors to join me in writing Creating Good Work, we did so through human contact with one another and our desire to shift intransigence around pressing social issues. As it turned out, The Shambhala Principle informed every step we took. And from those initial conversations, an opportunity to inform others took place. And from those interactions, there were still others that emerged. The chain of adjacency extends on and makes a difference with every interaction. That is the nature of a principle, it applies whether you are aware of it or not.

# From Self to Social Collaboration

Within the world of social entrepreneurship, there has been a focus on scaling programs to meet the needs of more and more people. This scaling effort has only had a limited effect to bring about the intention of the work being done. Part of the reason for this limitation is that scale is an industrial age term that is not applicable to human relationships or interactions. It aptly describes what takes place within the mechanical world, a world in which widgets are produced one after the other with little or no differentiation in how they are manufactured. Scaling of these efforts, which may range from being very simple to being quite complicated, do not accurately describe what takes place in the complex world of human interactions. Complex and complicated describe two very different kinds of worlds. Scale can take place in any environment in which the physical pieces can be brought together. Complex interactions and relationships are all situational and context-dependent. They take place within an environment that influences the interaction, whether those are prevailing cultural situations or coming out of specific ways of thinking about the world.

When we are involved in complex interactions, whether we are relating to only one other person or to many, something emerges out of those interactions that is greater than the sum of the parts and is not contained alone within the parts. Complex interactions are for the most part bio-based, non-mechanical, non-linear and take place among complex adaptive systems. Since social entrepreneurs, being human complex adaptive systems, are involved in interactive relational efforts, as opposed to the mechanical processes of manufacturing, scaling operations is simply not an effective description of what is taking place. Perhaps a better term for describing and growing these social interactive efforts is, reach. Reach is defined here as an extension from self toward other. In making that effort, it is an invitation to meet and join and relate within a mutual interaction, and toward that end, form a social collaboration.

While there may be many more ingredients within the interactive soup from which our reach emerges, there are three essential elements that help describe the extension of our reach beyond the self toward Other. They are: Encounter, Engagement, and Enactment. However, at any point within this interactive system, rejection can surface and derail the entire effort of the process. But, when these three elements are effectively applied, our reach can be extended toward the development, goals, and objections we envision. It is within this reach toward other that we move from an individual effort to one embodied in relationships and interaction, and ultimately social collaboration.

But what do we mean by encounter, engagement, and enactment? Encounter is how we meet other, our willingness to be open to another and meet them, not just superficially, but at a level of connectedness that lowers our barriers and allows a genuine and authentic conversation to take place. This requires a level of self-awareness and mind-training to be able to show-up ready to encounter the Other. Our same old ways may not be enough to build the relationships required to extend our reach if we are stuck in old ways of thinking and we are unable to do the work required in encountering another. That work shows up in how we get to know one another.

We learn about each other through the stories we share about our life experiences. We learn how we relate to each other and the world through our reaction to those stories—do they keep us down, enliven our lives, limit our ability to develop, demonstrate our perception of humor, or our willingness to meet the world as it shows up? When the stories we tell about ourselves emerge from an open and friendly heart, we connect. That ability to connect and remain open to the goodness we find in that encounter with another readies us for the next step we must take together.

Traditionally, engagement is period of time that proceeds marriage. However, in this context, we are not necessarily looking for a lifelong commitment, although that might certainly emerge, but rather our commitment to work together to solve a problem that is bigger than either or any of us. In making this commitment to engage together, we form a bond and a responsibility toward the relationship that formed within our encounter together. This is the point when our willingness to interact comes together with our need to address the situation before us.

*Engagement* also implies our ability to change on a personal level, allow for change in others, and to make sure the changes we wish to bring to a system can be accommodated by that system. If the boundaries in which the system operates are neither resilient nor accommodating, any concerted effort could threaten the system in such a way that it rejects the effort, or is completely overpowered by it, and since its boundaries are not resilient enough to accommodate the change, it simply breaks apart.

The chaotic state that ensues requires a complete rebounding in order to affect the desired change. At these rather cathartic moments, a good deal of the old system is lost or dissipated, and something new needs to be reformed. However, within that reformation, we must be careful because at the moment of reforming we lock into the new system all its potential and limitations. If its potential outweighs its limitations, it can effectively reach out into the world and have a profound impact. If the limitations and potential equation is reversed, the system may be DOA—dead on arrival.

Engaging with others toward a better end is at the heart of our reaching beyond self toward Other. And we are seeing these collaborations happening in greater numbers, because they must. Engaging with others to meet the challenges we face is how we get this work done.

And finally, *Enactment* is doing the work that needs to be done. As our reach extends, more work needs to take place. We cannot neglect to take into account the situations or the context we encounter in each new iteration, because they will invariably shape and inform our activity, and we cannot limit our reaching out to others in our effort to develop and grow the work before us. The work cannot be done alone. The social collaboratives we enact and which become empowered need to continually reestablish the same kinds of resilient boundaries that have successfully supported earlier efforts. Unlike mechanical scaling operations, complex relation-based organizations need to be constantly diligent and sensitive to the environment in which they are operating and continually mindful of the conditions that can affect the interactions taking place.

In the simple and complicated states, we can learn to accurately predict what we can expect from any future scaling. But unfortunately, the world of human complex interactions, doesn't afford that capability. Reaching out toward the other implies a level of unpredictability that can only be addressed through our recognition of the basic goodness each of us brings to our work. Joining those efforts into a collective response reaches into the hearts of each participant and from that relational connectivity, we are able to reach even further. In doing so we must, with every encounter, recognize and appreciate our inherent goodness, humanity and connection to other. It is what separates us from widgets and mechanical operations, and holds the promise of reaching the opportunities and solutions before us.

## Social Emergence:
## Aligning Interaction and Intention

**M**any years ago, Caltech made famous the notion, *Shift Happens*. We live in a world, on a planet where nothing is wholly stable or permanent. It's not the easiest of environments to create the illusion of balance and sustainability, or for that matter predictability. But we sure try, even though the only thing we can really count on is that when we least expect it, shift happens.

The good news is, that within that context, and at any given moment, change can take place. And what seems most intransigent is actually always ready to move. Dictators suddenly fall, economies collapse, bulbs rise from frozen soil, people work together to make their lives more livable.

The manifestation of change is emergence—which in and of itself is not necessarily good or bad, positive or negative—it simply takes place. Two or more living agents interact, and out of that interaction something emerges that is greater than the sum of the parts, and not wholly contained within either. The key aspect here is that for emergence/change to take place, living things need to interact, then shift happens. And out of this shifting comes the idea of *social emergence*. Now it would be safe to declare that, since living things have to interact for emergence to take place, that social emergence is something akin to the Department of Redundancy Department. But the distinction being made here is that within the arena of society, and our attempts to change society to make it more livable, social emergence is an effort to describe and explain the phenomena that is possible when conscious individuals interact. Actually, I don't want to open up a debate on consciousness; so let's simply say, when humans interact.

In societies around the globe, the social bi-polarism that arises when it comes to acknowledging anyone who might hold a different point of view is pervasive, even among people who essentially believe the same thing. This is true whether we are discussing religious differences, political decisions or academic thinking. I recently facilitated an ISCE conference that took place in one of the most beautiful cities on earth, Paris. Amid all that beauty, the conference, with attendees whose main disagreement was based on a debate that often seemed to focus on the minutia of minutia, could also be characterized as being filled with pettiness, ego, and personal bluster. This was not about dialogue between brilliant minds that might actually create a new way of thinking among them, but something akin to a peacock strutting contest, with no prize other than self-aggrandizement. However, within the groups that were able to move beyond this academic backstabbing, real dialogue generated a deepening and furthering of the conversation, out of which a new level of understanding co-emerged. Within those groups unable to get beyond who was right, in which the operative expression was, "I would argue that," little or nothing new emerged beyond, perhaps, a heightened sense of aggression and self-righteousness.

The US Congress is another place where, a similar inability to have a human conversation between any two people who might disagree, has ground all possibility for social interaction to a dead halt. At a time when our world is begging for new thinking that can carry us forward without destroying all of us in the progression, we need to turn to the idea of social emergence—conversations not based on whether we agree, but on how we are aligned.

Social Emergence requires our interaction. It requires us to stop bickering over who is right, which is an argument that is wholly based on ego, and find areas on which we are aligned, so we can interact together and produce the solutions to the problems our bickering has gotten us into. They are problems, not challenges. And the only means we have that won't destroy what we are trying to preserve is our ability to speak with one another, our ability to get over our need to be right, our willingness to re-enshrine civility.

Now, I admit, I have my opinions and I will be the first to pass judgment on behavior that doesn't jibe with my sense of propriety. But that doesn't mean I am operating in the best interest of others. In fact, I am often chastised by more than my wife for being inappropriately uncompromising. I can guarantee that when I am locked in the throes of my me-ness and my righteous rightness, there is absolutely no positive social emergence because there is no interaction with the other taking place, and that means nothing changes. There is no relationship, problems go unsolved, and disagreement reigns from on top of a mountain of ego. In my mind, I may be right, but that and $1.95 will get you coffee at Starbucks.

Our ability to facilitate a socially emergent conversation, to propagate positive and effective Social Emergence, to surface something new, and how that might make a real difference in how we live this life, doesn't mean we stop disagreeing or think differently. It means we recognize that our willingness to meet within our diversity produces something greater than me in the mix. In this day and age, that's a tough one for many of us who would rather not talk about it, but would prefer to shoot it out with anyone threatening their me-ness.

Addressing the problems we face comes in our ability to relate to the other. Our humanity emerges in our encounter, engagement, and our willingness to work together. But, as killer tornadoes destroy lives and mobile homes across what we call our heartland, and superstorms flood our coasts, we can't seem to find a way to align against our own destruction. As millions die in wars over insignificant thoughts that we have solidified to justify the destruction, and billions live without clean water, or food to feed themselves and their families, we still can't align around solutions we could find together that could emerge beyond our need to be right.

Social emergence requires nothing from us expect to be open to the other and interact together. What comes from that interaction is not guaranteed to be good or bad. But until we start talking with each other rather than at each other, the problems that emerge within our social fabric will be overcome by our limitations rather than filled with the potential of the human opportunity. Whenever an organization is formulated and its limitations outweigh its potential, the organization fails and the system dies. It may be too late for any form of social emergence to counter-balance the centuries of conflict we have perpetrated on our own social organizational systems. But shift happens. And where intransigence suddenly melts, there's now the opportunity for a similar conversation to produce a more peaceful world.

Perhaps, just perhaps, our ability to interact around what aligns us rather than our need to be right can help us reformulate our organizations so that our potential outweighs our limitations, and we can make this life more livable for all of us.

# Tools for Thought

I n an innovative, non-linear world in which capturing and operationalizing interaction and emergence are central to gaining a competitive advantage, we need tools that can free us from linear thoughts and ideas that keep us stuck in our outdated, mechanistic models. It is little wonder then that we have witnessed a surge in mindfulness programs that offer a means and practice for breaking those bonds. But our attachments to linear, fixed ideas are deeply seeded. Our prejudices and biases for mechanisms over relationships, for predictability over the messiness of complexity, often overwhelm our ability to discern what to accept and what to reject.

I recently posed to a gathering of business people, a 5-minute distraction-free challenge, a test of one's ability to simply sit quietly without being distracted by cellphones, iPads, or for that matter any form of entertainment. For many, 5 minutes without distraction seems impossible. How about trying 90 seconds? How can we hope to change our fixed notions to deal more effectively in a non-linear world if our minds are so easily and continually distracted?

I once heard a speaker describe a very severe form of Attention Deficit Disorder he had. He called it ADOS— Attention Deficit, Oh Shiny!

As the space in which our processes and operations take place have become more complex, it should not be too surprising that our attention deficit has also increased. Nonetheless, capturing what emerges from within complex interactions requires a relative comfort with being able to just hang-out in space. And to most of us, that's a terrifying place to be. This, of course, explains why we are so quickly drawn to something different and shiny.

As soon as many of us encounter space, our first instinct is to fill it. Look at the environmental problems we've created for our world. Waste and sludge are seeping into our water supplies. Our houses are filled with stuff that is then discarded for even more stuff. The consequence, our landfills are over-filled with our ever increasing wasted stuff. Our need to fill space may very well push us off-planet to find more space we can fill.

As a case in point, my wife and I just returned from Santa Fe, NM where for the past eleven years our storage unit has held our own stuff that we could no longer fit in our house, but with which we couldn't possibly part. It has been said that our only possessions are our attachments. Letting go of those fixed possessions, which include our biased and prejudiced thoughts and ideas, means that we have to do something different. We have to find a means to end our habitual idea-based pack-rattedness.

In spite of our terror of empty space, it is just that place where we have to be willing to rest in order to break free from the ideas that keep us tied to a past that, in many cases, is really not worth preserving.

What does it take? It starts by sitting down, turning off all buzzes and bells desperately notifying us about the next great distraction, and simply breathing. Feeling the body breathe in and out. Once you can do that, the objective is equally direct. Don't hold on to the thoughts that arise. That doesn't mean try and stop the thoughts that come-up, just don't grab on to them and make them yet another possession.

What takes place as we get better at doing this is that we begin to find some space between the continual stream of thoughts and ideas we're generating. Initially, it may be the tiniest of spaces, but the more we do it, the more the space grows. And as we become more accomplished in this practice, our fear of the space also begins to dissipate and we discover that it actually makes us feel really good to have all that space around us.

Retailers have known this. Go into a multi-story shopping mall and you will frequently find that the area that often houses the most expensive stores is the one that has the greatest open space around it. Why? Because people feel better in those more spacious zones and subsequently feel more inclined to spend. As I mentioned earlier, being comfortable in the space allows us to know what to accept and reject and not be unconsciously lulled into habitual patterns.

Being secure and at ease in non-linear space, provides a tremendous advantage over those who would rather run from it. It means we are able to see clearly what is arising in the space from all the interactions around us. We can recognize the cues the environment is providing that point in the direction we should be looking. This spatial awareness is crucial for us to operate in complex situations. Without it, the very least that could happen is that we miss an opportunity that emerges. In the worst case, say a police officer confronting a rapidly unfolding crisis, it can mean the senseless loss of life.

The same way of thinking that in previous eras allowed us to operate in the world of the simple and complicated does not work within today's complex, non-linear world. It requires that we take different steps, to learn to let go of that old way of thinking. The answer is as simple as taking a seat and feeling yourself do what is about as natural as breathing. In fact it is breathing. The hard part is not running to the phone or tablet when it beckons us with the allure of a new shiny distraction.

Want to be a warrior in the world of non-linear complex interactions? Then you better learn to be the next great space-pilot, so you can navigate this emerging world with confidence and effectiveness. Sit down and don't hold on.

# Mindful Collaboration:
## The Path to Happiness and
## Good Business

I t's no secret that Steven Jobs, arguably the most creative innovator of our lifetime, practiced mindfulness. What he knew was that the more we are able to abandon ideas we hold tightly to, the better we can see with fresh eyes what might be right in front of us. The more we can listen to ourselves and others the less likely we are to get distracted from the tasks before us. And the better we are at perceiving markets and emerging opportunities, the more success we can realize for ourselves and others.

Unfortunately, visions of going viral push us in directions that are often counter to where we really want to go. We see videos on YouTube with hundreds of thousands of hits that boggle the imagination with their mindlessness. In contrast, brilliant presentations of well thought out ideas about how to change social challenges are all but ignored.

Reaching an audience and then seeing it increase is one of our most valued measures of success. It's a measurement that has no regard to content. The thinking is simple: the more popular the better. Pop culture is designed to be superfluous, it is built and then collapses around the vocabulary of fad, wave, trend, craze, vogue, style, and fashion.

Organizations are certainly not immune. Plotting and scheming to move from a group to a movement is the dream of every changemaker. And to prove it, billions of dollars are spent each year to market and magnetize people to the next big thing. However, our culture of wanting more often overlooks why we want more. The answer to that is fairly simple: happiness. We've even started developing ways of measuring happiness, and what we discover is that we aren't all that happy, but we sure want to be.

Our unhappiness is what drives us to search for that great new idea that promises us fashion, fame and fortune. And even though we know happiness is rarely found in lasting measure in any of those things, we aren't sure where else to look. For many, the drive to move beyond the *three F's* can become a source of disappointment. "How can I ever hope to change the world for the better, alone?" We see evidence of those that have; Gandhi, Martin Luther King, Florence Nightingale, Pete Seeger, Aung San Suu Kyi, Muhammad Yunus, but is that really who *we* are?

Then we hear about the emergence of social entrepreneurs who are actually doing well by doing good. This idea starts resonating in ways that make complete sense with both who we are and what we want to bring to the world. But the thought of starting, alone, feels overwhelming.

The fact is, of course, that none of these folks, from Gandhi to Yunus, did what they did alone. They all recognized two things:

1.  They had to collaborate, and;

2.  They had to be willing to lead by example.

Collaborating with others begins with being sensitive to the current situation and environment in which we intend to operate. That sensitivity is not just to the environment outside, but to that within ourselves, as well. But if we aren't familiar with the terrain in either place, moving beyond our borders becomes even more challenging. This is especially true when we're trying to work with others.

To breakthrough that boundary, we make inquiries into and about our local landscape , that place we share together. Not too surprisingly, from this interaction a call to action often arises. This is not necessarily one of those dramatic cloud-parting callings with thunder and lightning, although if that shows up, it's best to listen. Usually, it starts with a feeling, an intuition, an appreciation for what has to be done. And we know we have to do it.

The critical factor is listening to it, however it emerges. In listening for this calling, we are developing a mindfulness about the current conditions that surround us.

The truth is, this is not an unknown place to many of us. We often find ourselves in mindful states: when we're showering, walking down the street, going shopping, or exercising. When we space out doing these things, something invariably makes us aware that we've lost our focus and brings us back, like tripping over a curb, or forgetting the bread you went to the market for in the first place. Mindfulness and awareness are nothing more than that, focusing on something specific and becoming aware when you've become distracted from it and are brought back.

Another means for cultivating both mindfulness and awareness is meditation. Meditation is nothing more than looking at what arises as we sit without distraction and then bring our focus back to our meditation. If we space out and, metaphorically speaking, trip over something in our way , we return to our focus. The outcome is we eventually learn that even when we are not meditating, we are still able to continue to focus our attention on the current conditions around us, which often leads us to an encounter we might otherwise have not seen or predicted.

Being willing to encounter someone and have a real conversation is a first step toward collaboration and the innovation that can arise out of those interactions. Now, we've all had conversations that didn't lead to working together with someone, as well as those in which something totally unexpected emerged. Human interactions are simply unpredictable. We have no way to accurately know what will emerge when people interact.

However, when we are unable or unwilling to recognize this unpredictability, we lose all ability to find common ground. Instead we focus on the disappointment of our unfulfilled expectation, and rather than reaching out toward another, we become even more self-absorbed in dissatisfaction. Effective collaboration depends on our ability to connect more directly with others and ourselves. When it comes to making a genuine impact on the world we encounter, mindfulness—our ability to connect with ourselves and be open to others—is a key component in how we get there.

The mindfulness required to recognize our own sense of worthiness, and then reach out toward others, requires more than just a wish to do so. It requires our being willing to look at ourselves and how we show-up. Why is this important? Because mindfulness is about being present, and it is while we are present that we can see and capture what emerges out of our conversations and collaborations, together. Without the ability to be present with ourselves and others, no real exchange can take place. And if there's no exchange taking place then we're not really collaborating.

If we're not really collaborating, then nothing truly novel is emerging that can magnetize others to join our collaboration, and by extension, create even greater interaction and subsequent emergence. And since the most effective and productive collaborations take place when we are truly mindful of ourselves and others, it stands to reason that we reach more people by cultivating it than by ignoring it.

That's how we make lasting change and start movements that aren't simply the next big thing. And, oh yes, how we begin to generate real happiness. The question is, are we willing to incorporate into our programs what corporations all over the country are recognizing; that cultivating mindfulness is good for everyone and good business.

# Assessing a Healthy Economy with Gross National Happiness

I n building a healthy economy, what we measure and evaluate is crucial to demonstrating aspiration, progress, and success. Traditional economic indicators just don't tell the whole picture. The state of Vermont has recognized this. They have adopted a growing trend toward assessing its population's well-being. The *Vermont well-being survey* clearly states: "The way forward toward a new economy of well-being: measure what matters. What you measure is what you get. So, we better measure what we want to get."

What Vermont and other regions around the world are now measuring falls under the larger title of Gross National Happiness—the health and well-being of its citizens. Now, this is not a slightly veiled Occupy-like reaction to materialists who focus solely on Gross National Product to determine our economic temperature. It's a means of truly tapping into the pulse of a nation, its values and its real satisfaction.

Those seeming intangibles translate directly and tangibly, according to the UN's World Happiness Report 2013, into such things as longer life expectations, higher earnings potentials and higher productivity levels. Jeffrey Sachs, co-editor and director of Columbia University's Earth Institute, was quoted in an article in the Digital Journal and made the point:

> *There is now a rising worldwide demand that policy be more closely aligned with what really matters to people as they themselves characterize their well-being. The World Happiness Report 2013 offers rich evidence that*

*the systematic measurement and analysis of happiness*
*can teach us a lot about ways to improve the world's*
*well-being and sustainable development.*

In addition, according to the *OECD Guidelines on Measuring Subjective Well-Being,*

*Measures of subjective well-being provide an alternative*
*yardstick of progress that is firmly grounded in people's*
*experiences [...] In particular, being grounded in peoples'*
*experiences and judgments on multiple aspects of their*
*life, measures of subjective well-being are uniquely*
*placed to provide information on the net impact of*
*changes in social and economic conditions on the*
*perceived well-being of respondents, taking into account*
*the impact of differences in tastes and preferences*
*among individuals.*

We are now seeing more and more municipalities cultivating indicators of well-being to assess their greater social and economic health. Many of these same cities, like Seattle, WA, Santa Monica, CA and Houston, TX, are also signatories to the *Charter for Compassion*. By signing this document, they pledge to make their municipality a city of compassion. Compassion, health and well-being are distinct indicators of our satisfaction and happiness.

In taking these steps toward greater health and well-being, cities, states and countries are not just falling in line with the latest trend. They are recognizing the conversation has to change. The satisfaction, well-being and compassion of those living within any defined border are not just something to give lip-service to or to become the butt of a condescending joke. They must be seriously addressed, acted upon and implemented for the sake of the greater good of the region. A healthy economy is one where the measure of its vibrancy is not only characterized by a dollar sign.

The history of Gross National Happiness (GNH) began in the country of Bhutan in 1972, where the term was first coined by Bhutan's fourth Dragon King, Jigme Singye Wangchuck. He did this as a way of shifting the economy of his nation from the more conventional measures to one he felt better suited the spiritual nature of his country.

In defining GNH, four pillars were established.

1.  The promotion of equitable and sustainable socio-economic development;

2.  The preservation and promotion of cultural values;

3.  The conservation of the natural environment, and;

4.  The establishment of good governance.

These four pillars were then translated into nine domains. In Vermont, a tenth was added. As with any index, by assessing individuals across each of the prescribed domains a more complete picture of their happiness and well-being, as well as that of the overall region, emerges. The domains according to the Vermont survey are:

**1.    Psychological well-being:** The degree of satisfaction and optimism within an individual's life, analyzing self-esteem, sense of competence, stress, spiritual activities, and the prevalence of positive and negative emotions.

**2.  Health:** How effective are health policies? This looked at such things as self-rated healthiness, disabilities, patterns of risk behavior, exercise, sleep and nutrition.

**3.  Use of Time:** This element is significant in assessing the quality of life. How much time is spent on recreation and socializing with family and friends? Finding a balance in how we manage time included such things as work hours, time spent in traffic jams, and improving one's education.

**4.  Community Vitality:** How engaged is the individual with others? What are their relationships to others and their community? Indicators are personal confidence, a sense of belonging and worth, the depth of affection they feel, the security of their home and community, and how that translated into more generous efforts like volunteering and giving.

**5.  Education:** This domain measures the individual's actual participation in formal and informal education, the development of skills and associated capabilities, involvement in children's education, values education, as well as environmental education pursuits.

**6.  Culture:** The focus here is on evaluating local traditions, festivals, core values, participation in cultural events, opportunities to develop artistic skills, and if the individual has experienced any discrimination due to religion, race or gender.

**7.  Environment:** This domain is about the individual's relationship to the physical world in which they live. It takes into account the perception of the quality of the water, air, soil, forest cover, and the biodiversity of the area.

**8.    Governance:** What is the view of government, the media, the judiciary system, the electoral system, and the police? This is measured in terms of responsibility, honesty and transparency. It also looks at an individual's involvement in community decision making and political processes.

**9.    Standard of Living:** A traditional economic measure of individual and family income, financial security, the level of debt, employment security and the quality of housing in which the individual and their family lives.

**10.    Working Life:** (Experimental Domain added by Vermont in the 2012 Happiness Initiative GNH survey) This domain evaluates the connection between work and identity, a key component of well-being. How does the individual feel about time spent at work?

In building a healthy economy, we're not interested in simply building and selling more. We have to be able to gauge the real level of satisfaction, engagement and compassion we have toward each other. These are what truly fill this life with value and worth.

Happiness is not based on material possessions or the wealth generated by local businesses. It's our connection to ourselves and others. Real satisfaction and meaning emerge when we recognize our interdependence and what that means in terms of how we treat one another and want to be treated. Creating good work and building a healthy economy are not just things we dream about. They are what we must do to realize the happiness available to any of us willing to work for it.

# Onward

As those who have ever received a note from me over the years are well aware, I use the exclamation, *Onward,* to close my thoughts and acknowledge the path ahead.

Onward from here is not about what will be or where I've been, it's about knowing that the ground and path are being covered and fruition is always one breath away. It's about a commitment to act for the benefit of others, to not leave because what shows-up is challenging, but rather to understand that it's all workable. That's a tough one.

I have no illusions about the future. I try to limit my hope. I do know that if we can initiate healthy interactions with everyone we encounter, we will make a better world. I also know there are lots of folks who are unable to act from a place of health. I also know that their suffering invariably begets even more suffering, especially when it's pushed onto others.

The great and wonderful Khandro Rinpoche said in her book, *This Precious Life*, "Suffering is meeting every moment absolutely capable of transforming it and not taking the opportunity to do so."

In the cosmos of Complexity and Buddhist thought there is no separation. Everything is interdependent and only exists as it does because of something else. And in the possibility space that surrounds us there is great laughter, love, and opportunity. How we meet it is our choice. My longing is to meet it exactly as it is.

As direct evidence of this, Thomas Tran Dinh, a survivor of the horrific attack on the Bataclan in Paris, in which more than 90 died, said to a reporter on MSNBC:

*It's easy to succumb to hate and fear and when I got out the first thing I thought about were my loved ones. There's no possibility for hate, then. I don't feel revenge... I think the message is to love each other. It is easy to have hate... We need to love each other.*

May we benefit many.